Josy Argy is a former editor of *Woman's Realm*, and Wendy Riches was her assistant editor on the magazine.

Now freelance journalists, they first became interested in the English Tourist Board's 'Taste of England' scheme to promote real English food when they spotted the Board's symbol on a traditional menu in a Bath restaurant. They contacted the Board and decided to write a book about the 'Taste of England', after which they spent a happy six months travelling around the country sampling local dishes and gathering recipes – all of which they then tried out on their lucky families and friends.

The result is a unique and fascinating cookbook/guidebook that will delight those who already love real English food – and amaze those who think that our national culinary heritage is limited to meat and two veg!

Also by Josy Argy and Wendy Riches in Sphere Books
BRITAIN'S ROYAL BRIDES

A Taste of England

JOSY ARGY & WENDY RICHES

SPHERE BOOKS LIMITED
30/32 Gray's Inn Road, London WC1X 8JL

First published by Sphere Books Ltd 1979
Copyright © Josy Argy & Wendy Riches 1979

FOR GRANNIE TOWNSHEND, TO WHOM WE OWE SO MUCH

Printed in Great Britain by
Hazell Watson & Viney Ltd
Aylesbury, Bucks

CONTENTS

ACKNOWLEDGMENTS

We would like to thank the English Tourist Board, and in particular Jackie Gurney, for their co-operation, and the chefs, hoteliers and restaurateurs for sharing their recipes with us. And a special thank you to Hilary Wills for her charming illustrations.

INTRODUCTION

Good English food is wonderful; bad English food is awful. The reason is simple; unlike our Continental neighbours, we are traditionally plain cooks and many of our classic dishes depend on first-class ingredients: prime beef, pork and lamb, fresh fish from sea and river, a wide selection of game and the produce of orchards and market gardens.

Our forefathers, who lived and ate well, made the most of these. Then two world wars, years of rationing and shortages left their mark on English eating habits.

Today, however, there is a resurgence of interest in good English food, and regional specialities based on fresh local produce are coming back into their own, both in restaurants and in family cooking.

The English Tourist Board – through their 'Taste of England' promotion – have done much to awaken public interest in a rich culinary heritage. Close on eight hundred restaurants now belong to the scheme, all offering English food prepared in the traditional way. (The official guide is available from the English Tourist Board, 4 Grosvenor Gardens, London SW1W 0DU, or from larger Tourist Information Centres. There are more than 360 Tourist Information Centres throughout England, all identified by a blue and white sign with the letter 'i' on it. They can give information on local events, activities and accommodation as well as general holiday advice.)

From these eight hundred we have made our own – of necessity smaller – selection. This book is the result: over a hundred restaurants where you will find a warm welcome, good food and comfortable surroundings.

They range from country inns to restaurants housed in stately homes; from guest houses to luxury hotels, and each one has generously shared its recipes with us, and with you. In the following pages you will find over a hundred and ninety dishes to try for yourself. There are delicious ways with pheasant, guinea fowl and salmon along with many dishes using inexpensive, everyday ingredients – like creamy Brussels Sprouts Soup, Cidered Pork, Cheese and Apple Casserole, Spring Greens Pie and a lovely hot pudding – Ginger Royal.

We have recipes from the past. The Tate Gallery in London, Truffles in Manchester and the Hen and Chicken Inn in Alton, Hampshire, are just three of a number of places doing research into old recipes and bringing them up to date. And you will find regional dishes from the twelve areas which make up England in the book. Rum Nicky from Cumbria, Yorkshire Cheesecake, Likkypie from Cornwall, Thame Tart from Oxfordshire, Shropshire Fidget Pie and Bakewell Tart.

We couldn't leave out old favourites like Bakewell Tart and we make no excuses for giving as many as three versions of Steak and Kidney Pie – two quite different ways of making this traditional dish and the third a delicious *cold* version. But you will also find many new, unusual and imaginative recipes for we have taken a broad view of English food.

Cookery is a living craft, affected by the factors which make up our daily lives. Foreign travel, an influx of immigrants and tourists and exciting foreign foods have all influenced the way we eat today, just as the Empire and the Colonies did years ago. And in this country now there are a number of international restaurateurs who have made a lasting contribution to our way of eating.

We hope you will enjoy the book and the food. All the recipes are simple to make, many are quick, others can be made in advance. Each one has been tested in our own kitchens.

Quantities are in Imperial measures, approximate metric equivalents and American cups and spoons. But we have taken a commonsense view. If a chef specifies a tablespoon or a teaspoon and the small variation between British and US sizes makes no difference to the success of the recipe, we have not given alternatives.

We have followed the English Tourist Board's method of price coding for the restaurants:

A – a 3-course meal for under £3 per person
B – a price range of £3–£5 per person
C – prices over £5 per person
 (This does not include drinks)

Eating out is part of the pleasure of a touring holiday. We hope you will find the restaurants as good as we did. But eating is a subjective business and the food industry is particularly vulnerable. So let's hope the restaurant hasn't changed hands, pray the manager hasn't moved and keep our fingers crossed that the chef isn't having a bad evening . . .

Josy Argy
Wendy Riches

CUMBRIA
The County of Cumbria

SHEILA'S COTTAGE (A, B)

The Slack, Ambleside, Cumbria
Tel: Ambleside 3079
Open 10 am to 5 pm; 6.30 pm to 8 pm (last orders)
Closed on Sunday and during January and February

This charming seventeenth-century Westmorland cottage in the centre of Ambleside offers an imaginative selection of country dishes, including a number of regional specialities. It's inviting from the outside, the old stone a good background for colourful window boxes and climbers, and cosy inside, which still has the original flag floor.

At lunchtime there is a selection of fresh salads and cold platters, home-made soup followed by home-baked cakes and pastries. Teatime can produce local specialities like Grasmere Gingerbread and fresh scones served with home-made damson jam. The evening menu, served from 6.30 pm, offers an interesting choice of dishes – with usually two or three starters including home-made soup and cream cheese with fresh herbs, with home-made Cumbrian oatcakes and celery. The main course is provided by a choice of two oven-to-table dishes changed each night – we give you the recipe for Westmorland Tatie Pot; and the puddings always include a regional speciality like Cumberland Rum Nicky.

Like so many successful hotels and restaurants which combine good food with a personal touch, Sheila's Cottage is run by a husband and wife team – in this case Jan and Stewart Greaves.

RECIPES FROM SHEILA'S COTTAGE

Westmorland 'Tatie Pot'

For 4 people
  2 lb (960 g) *stewing lamb*
  2 *medium onions*

I

1 large carrot
4 medium tomatoes or a small can Italian peeled tomatoes
2 tablespoons dripping or oil
1 heaped tablespoon plain flour
1 pint (0·57 litres 2⅓ cups) water or stock
1 black pudding
1 lb (480 g) potatoes
salt, freshly-milled black pepper
a little butter

Trim fat off the meat and fry it in the oil or dripping until nicely browned. Using a slotted spoon, transfer the meat to a casserole. Sauté the roughly chopped onion and carrot in the fat until soft and brown. Add the chopped, skinned tomatoes or the can of peeled tomatoes and cook for a minute or two. Stir in the flour to soak up the juices and gradually add the stock or hot water. Keep stirring over heat until it forms a thickish gravy. Thinly slice the black pudding and put a layer on top of the meat. Pour the gravy on top. Peel and thinly slice the potatoes and put in layers over the meat and gravy. Season each layer of potatoes with salt and pepper and scatter small knobs of butter in between. Cover casserole and cook slowly in the oven at Gas Mark 2 (300°F/150°C) for about 2 hours. Take the cover off for the last half hour to brown the potatoes. Check during cooking; sometimes a little more stock needs to be added as the potatoes absorb some of the gravy. This very filling dish is traditionally served with pickled red cabbage or chutney.

Cumberland Rum Nicky

For 6–8 people
The pastry:
    8 oz (240 g/2 cups) plain flour
    2 oz (60 g/4 tablespoons) lard and 2 oz (60 g/4 tablespoons) margarine
      or 4 oz (120 g/½ cup) butter
    water to mix

The filling:
    6 oz (180 g/1 cup) chopped dates
    6 oz (180 g) Bramley apple – 1 large one
    2 oz (60 g/⅓ cup) chopped preserved ginger
    2 oz (60 g/4 tablespoons) butter

2 oz (60 g/⅓ cup) soft brown sugar
2 tablespoons rum

This delicious pie is a traditional Cumbrian recipe. Make the pastry by rubbing the fats into the flour and binding with cold water. Roll out and line a flan ring. Prick the bottom. Make the filling by beating the brown sugar with the butter, add the rum, then the chopped dates, the peeled, cored and chopped apple and the ginger. Put this mixture in the flan, make a trellis pattern over it from left-over pastry and bake at Gas Mark 5 (375°F/190°C) for about 30 minutes. Serve warm with fresh whipped cream.

PARKEND RESTAURANT (B)

Parkend, Caldbeck, Wigton, Cumbria
Tel: Caldbeck 442
Open 12 noon to 2 pm (last orders); 7 pm to 9 pm (last orders)
Closed Mondays and throughout January and February

Set in beautiful countryside among the Cumbrian fells, this family-run restaurant offers freshly-cooked food in charming surroundings. What was once a seventeenth-century farmhouse has been skilfully converted to retain the cosy rural feeling; the restaurant has a low beamed ceiling and partly exposed thick stone walls.

You choose from a 4- or 5-course set dinner or make your own selection from the bill of fare. Lunch can be a light snack at the bar or a 3-course meal. The menu carries Cumbrian specialities and unusual home-made soups like the subtly-flavoured Lettuce and Watercress Soup for which we give you the recipe. The restaurant seats 30 and it is advisable to book for dinner.

RECIPE FROM PARKEND RESTAURANT

Lettuce and Watercress Soup

For 4 people
   1 head of lettuce or the outer leaves of several
   1 bunch watercress
   1 medium onion, finely chopped

3

1 oz (30 g/2 tablespoons) butter
1 oz (30 g/¼ cup) flour
1½ pints (0·85 litres/4 cups) chicken stock
salt and pepper
1 egg yolk
½ pint (0·28 litres/1¼ cups) double cream
chopped mint or grated nutmeg

Shred the lettuce and strip the thick stalks from the watercress. Wash both well. Melt the butter in a pan, add the onion and the lettuce and watercress, cook gently for about 5 minutes. Draw aside and blend in the flour. Bring the chicken stock (you can use stock cubes) to the boil and pour onto the lettuce; season with salt and freshly ground pepper. Simmer for 15–20 minutes. Then sieve or liquidise. Return to the pan. Beat the egg yolk and cream together and add to the soup. Re-heat gently, being careful not to boil. Serve sprinkled with chopped mint or grated nutmeg. This is a delicious soup, just as nice to have chilled on a summer's evening.

AYNSOME MANOR HOTEL (C)

Cartmel, Grange-over-Sands, Cumbria
Tel: Cartmel 276
Open 7 pm to 9 pm (last orders 8.30 pm)
Sunday lunch 1 pm
Closed Sunday evening and Christmas bank holiday (except for residents)

'We aim to provide a home-from-home by cooking good food the way it should be and serving it in a pleasant and informal manner,' says Alan Williams, proprietor of the Aynsome Manor Hotel.

'We sometimes wonder if we've gone too far when our regulars stroll into the kitchen and join us for breakfast. Recently someone turned up in the kitchen at 7.45 in the morning saying he couldn't sleep and actually helped us to cook breakfast!'

Alan runs the hotel with his wife Sue and his sister-in-law Jill. They share the cooking – the two recipes we give you are their personal favourites; Alan's is the Cheese and Onion Soup and Sue's is the Loin of Pork with Pâté.

Aynsome Manor, situated in the beautiful Vale of Cartmel, was the residence of the descendants of William Marshal, Earl of Pembroke, who founded historic Cartmel Priory in 1188. Today there are thirteen bedrooms, seven with private bath en suite, a cosy bar and two charming lounges with views over the valley. Across the hotel's cobbled courtyard lies Aynsome Cottage, recently converted to provide three double bedrooms, all with private bathrooms, and a comfortable lounge.

RECIPES FROM AYNSOME MANOR HOTEL

Cheese and Onion Soup

For 6–8 people
6–8 onions
4 pints (2·28 litres/10⅔ cups) chicken stock
1 pint (0·57 litres/2⅔ cups) milk
6 oz (180 g/1½ cups) Cheddar cheese, grated
1½–2 oz (45–60 g/3–4 tablespoons) butter
1½–2 oz (45–60 g/⅓–½ cup) flour
salt and freshly ground pepper
chopped parsley for garnish

Peel and slice the onions and boil in the chicken stock. Make a pint of cheese sauce using the milk, butter and flour and the Cheddar cheese. When the onions are cooked, slowly add them and the stock to the cheese sauce a little at a time, blending the stock smoothly into the cheese sauce. Add salt and pepper to taste and a little fresh parsley. The result is a creamy onion soup with a delicate cheese flavour.

Roast Loin of Pork stuffed with Pâté

For 6 people
A 4-lb (1·920 kg) pork loin, boned, skinned and trimmed of excess fat
3 oz (90 g) chicken liver pâté (preferably home-made)
3 oz (90 g) mushrooms, washed and sliced
a little brandy
2 eggs
pinch of sage; salt and black pepper
4 oz (120 g/1⅓ cups) fresh breadcrumbs

a little milk
3 tablespoons flour
a little vegetable stock

Lay the loin fat side down on a wooden board; sprinkle with salt, sage and freshly ground black pepper. In a basin, combine the pâté with 1 egg and $\frac{1}{4}$ of the breadcrumbs, spread over the loin. Layer the mushrooms along the centre of the loin, pour over a little brandy. Roll up the meat and tie securely with string at 1-inch intervals. Place meat on a wire rack in a meat tin, with the join facing down. Brush with milk, then dust with flour. Leave for 10 minutes. Brush over with beaten egg and coat with breadcrumbs. Cook at Gas Mark 4 (350°F/180°C) for $1\frac{1}{2}$–2 hours or until cooked. Place meat in a clean meat tin and keep warm. Mix 2 tablespoons of plain flour with the meat juices and cook to a roux. Then slowly add a little vegetable stock to the required thickness. Slice the meat or leave whole; serve garnished with watercress with gravy in a separate boat.

THE PHEASANT INN (A, B)

Bassenthwaite Lake, Cockermouth, Cumbria
Tel: Bassenthwaite Lake 234
Open 12.30 pm to 2 pm; 7 pm to 8.30 pm
Closed Christmas Day

The Pheasant is exactly what most of us look for in a residential English country pub – sixteenth-century, trim black and white exterior; inside, the ancient all-wood bar with little tables, patterned curtains, smoke-mellowed walls, offering real ale and a warm welcome; comfortable lounges with chintz covered furniture, log fires and fresh flowers; spotless bedrooms – some in a cottage annexe – and good, country food served in a pleasant, beamed dining room. Add to this a magnificent Lakeland setting, with blue mountain peaks and dark green pines – and who could ask for more? It is a romantic venue at all times of the year, but specially in the spring and autumn when the trees are at their most dramatic.

Service in the pub is friendly and helpful, as with most places in Cumbria, and you are well placed for visiting the beauty spots in the Lake District, the Border country, and the quiet Cumbrian coast. But one of the nicest things to do on a sunny day is to take a packed picnic lunch (from the Pheasant's kitchens) and head for somewhere off the tourists' well-beaten tracks, in the peace of the surrounding hills.

RECIPES FROM THE PHEASANT

Braised Ox Tongue with Mushroom and Marsala Sauce

For 8–10 people
  A 4–5 lb (1·92–2·40 kg) pickled ox tongue
  about 10 oz (300 g) roughly chopped root vegetables (onion, carrots and celery)
  1 pint (0·57 litres/2⅔ cups) brown sauce (see recipe for it under Tripe and Onions, Drake's Restaurant, London section)
  about 2 pints (1·14 litres/5¼ cups) brown stock
  3 tablespoons Marsala
  5 oz (150 g) sliced button mushrooms
  beef dripping and a little butter for cooking
  salt and freshly-milled pepper

Wash the tongue and place on top of the chopped vegetables in a roasting tray. Smear with beef dripping and season well with salt and pepper. Fill tray to half way up the tongue with brown stock and cover tray securely with foil. Cook in a medium oven Gas Mark 4 (350°F/180°C) for 3–4 hours. Cool slightly, peel off the skin and remove the root of the tongue.
  Cut the cooked tongue into slices and arrange neatly on serving dish, cover with the sauce and sprinkle with finely chopped parsley.

The sauce:
Simmer 1 pint of brown sauce with a similar quantity of brown stock till reduced by half. Sauté the sliced mushrooms in butter in a separate pan for 2–3 minutes, add the Marsala then strain the sauce on the mushrooms. Simmer for a few minutes and check seasonings before serving.

Rum, Chocolate and Raisin Mousse

For 4–6 people
  about 4 oz (120 g/just under 1 cup) caster sugar
  4 eggs
  ½ pint (0·28 litres/1⅓ cups) double cream

4 leaves gelatine – or ½ oz (15 g/1½ tablespoons) powdered
⅓ pint (2·27 decilitres/just under 1 cup) milk
1½ dessertspoons cocoa powder
1 measure of rum
2 oz (60 g/⅓ cup) raisins

Separate the eggs. Whisk the yolks and the sugar with a touch of water till the mixture is pale and forms a ribbon. Keep on one side. Meanwhile heat the milk and the cocoa in a pan. Take off the stove and add the gelatine, softened in a little water. Leave in a cool place till nearly set. Soak the raisins in rum and add to the yolks and sugar mixture. Whip the cream, add to the mixture and stir. Whisk the egg whites and keep to one side whilst adding gelatine mix to rest of ingredients. Finally gently fold whites into mixture and pour into serving dishes. Chill in refrigerator and decorate with whipped cream and chocolate curls.

CROSBY LODGE HOTEL (B)

Crosby-on-Eden, Carlisle, Cumbria
Tel: Crosby-on-Eden 618
Open 7.45 am to 9.30 am; 12.30 pm to 1.45 pm; 7.30 pm to 9 pm
Closed Sunday evening and from Christmas Eve to mid-January

Built of mellow brick, Crosby Lodge with its castellated towers has the air of a small castle. It dates back to the end of the eighteenth century. Originally built as a farmhouse, it was later enlarged into an attractive country mansion.

Michael and Patricia Sedgwick bought it in 1970 as a private house and proceeded to turn it into the comfortable hotel it is today with eleven bedrooms (nine of them with bathrooms), central heating, large and comfortable reception rooms and a charming walled garden.

The Sedgwicks ran a restaurant in Carlisle for fourteen years before taking over Crosby Lodge. Michael Sedgwick is the chef with two assistants. He trained in London at Brown's Hotel and the Kensington Palace, then had a spell in Switzerland. Mrs Sedgwick is in charge of the sweet trolley, with the help of a girl she has trained herself. They offer a limited à la carte menu, but their table d'hôte is so good and has such a variety of international and traditional British fare that most people find something to tempt them. The bar menu also offers a wide range of snacks.

The hotel is only 4½ miles from the historic city of Carlisle with its castle and fine small cathedral. It is very convenient for the Lake District, the Scottish Lowlands and lovely stretches of Cumbria and Northumberland where you can still follow Hadrian's Wall.

RECIPES FROM CROSBY LODGE HOTEL

Poussin stuffed with Lemon, Thyme and Parsley with Madeira Sauce

For 6 people
6 poussins
1 oz (30 g/2 tablespoons) dripping
2 large onions, chopped
2 celery stalks, chopped
1 teaspoon fresh thyme
1 teaspoon fresh chopped parsley
the juice and zest of 2 lemons
1 lb (480 g) white breadcrumbs
2 whole eggs, beaten
salt and pepper
6 rashers of bacon

The sauce:
1 pint (0·57 litres/2⅔ cups) brown sauce (see recipe for it in Tripe and
  Onions, Drake's Restaurant, London section)
4 fl oz (1·13 decilitres/about ½ cup) Madeira

To garnish:
1 bunch watercress
asparagus spears
3 small blanched tomatoes
6 large mushrooms

Make the stuffing by frying the onion and celery in the dripping until soft; add the herbs, lemon juice and zest and blend over heat. Mix in as much of the breadcrumbs as you need to give a fairly solid consistency and bind with the eggs.

Wipe the poussins and fill them with the stuffing, tying up the back carefully. Brush them with melted butter, cover the breasts with the bacon and roast in the oven at Gas Mark 6 (400°F/200°C) for about an hour or until tender. Garnish with asparagus tips, tomato, mushrooms and watercress and serve with the Madeira sauce, made by adding the Madeira to the brown sauce.

If you prefer a less rich dish, make a gravy from the juices in the pan instead of the Madeira sauce.

Stilton Croquettes with Tomato Sauce

For 6 people
  8 oz (240 g/1 cup) unsalted butter
  8 oz (240g/2 cups) plain flour
  1 pint (0·57 litres/2⅔ cups) milk
  8 oz (240 g) Stilton cheese, finely grated and creamed
  3 celery stalks, finely chopped
  4 egg yolks

For frying:
  seasoned flour
  fresh white breadcrumbs
  2 or 3 whole beaten eggs
  vegetable oil or other fat for deep frying

Tomato sauce:
  1 onion
  2 medium tins peeled tomatoes
  salt and pepper
  sugar

For the croquettes make a really thick bechamel sauce with the butter, flour and milk and cook for a few minutes, stirring continuously. Beat in the egg yolks, then the creamed Stilton and finally the very finely chopped celery. Spread the mixture out on a tray and allow it to go cold. When it is firm, roll it into balls about 1 inch in diameter, coat with seasoned flour, then beaten egg and breadcrumbs. Deep fry until golden. Serve with the tomato sauce and garnish with watercress.

For the sauce, fry one finely chopped onion in either butter or oil, or a combination of the two. Add the tomatoes, salt and pepper and a pinch of sugar. Let the sauce simmer till reduced, sieve or put through a mouli, check seasoning and serve very hot.

Hazelnut Mousse with Chocolate Sauce

For 6 people
5 eggs, separated (you will only use 2 egg whites)
7 tablespoons sugar
1 pint (0·57 litres/2⅔ cups) milk
1 cup whipping cream
2 oz (60 g/⅔ cup) hazelnuts, shelled, roasted and ground
½ teaspoon vanilla essence
½ oz (15 g/1½ tablespoons) gelatine

The sauce:
6 oz (180 g) bitter chocolate
¼ pint (0·28 litres/1¼ cups) water
4 oz (120 g/½ cup) granulated sugar

Make a custard by beating the egg yolks with 4 tablespoons sugar. Add the scalded milk slowly to the beaten yolks, stirring constantly in a double saucepan over a low heat. Whip the cream and mix with the cooled custard, the ground hazelnuts and the vanilla essence. Beat 2 egg whites with 3 tablespoons sugar. Dissolve the gelatine in a cup of hot water and leave it to cool. Before it sets, add it and the beaten egg whites to the whipped cream mixture and pour into separate bowls or glasses, but do not fill each bowl more than ¾ full. Leave to set in a cold place.

Make the chocolate sauce by breaking the chocolate and melting it in a pan with the water over a low heat; when smooth add the sugar; when sugar has dissolved, bring to the boil and simmer with the lid off the pan for 10–15 minutes until sauce is rich, syrupy and of a coating consistency. Allow to cool.

Decorate mousse with extra whipped cream and top with chocolate sauce.

WHITE MOSS HOUSE (C)

Rydal Water, Grasmere, Cumbria
Tel: Grasmere 295
Dinner 7 pm for 7.30 pm
Closed on Wednesday

What better way to enjoy the beauty of the English Lakes than from an old Lakeland house offering comfort and seclusion, lovely views and delicious food?

White Moss House, at the heart of the Lake District overlooking Rydal Water, once belonged to the poet William Wordsworth. There are only five bedrooms, two with private bath, all individually furnished, centrally heated and double glazed.

Antique furniture, fresh flowers everywhere, books and magazines and a small choice menu which changes daily give the feeling of staying in a beautifully run private house.

The Butterworths, who own and run the hotel, love the area and know it well. They will help you to plan your drives or walks and will welcome you back in time for dinner, carefully planned and prepared by Jean Butterworth, whose interest in English country cooking is reflected in her well balanced menus.

Even more secluded is Brockstone, converted from two old Lakeland cottages to provide a kitchen/dining-room, lounge, bathroom and a choice of a double or twin-bedded room, five minutes by car from White Moss House. You have your own garden, gorgeous views and facilities to make your own Continental breakfast. Jean Butterworth provides tea and coffee and baskets with rolls, fruit juice, marmalade, etc. If you prefer a full cooked English breakfast, you drive or walk over to the big house where you also have dinner. The restaurant is closed on Wednesday, but the Butterworths will be glad to book you into recommended restaurants in the area.

RECIPES FROM WHITE MOSS HOUSE

Avocado and Smoked Salmon Mousse

For 6 people
2 large avocado pears

⅓ cup olive oil
2 tablespoons lemon juice
salt and white pepper to taste
2 tablespoons whipped cream
2 tablespoons mayonnaise
⅔ cup diced smoked salmon

Peel the avocados and remove the stones. Cream in the liquidiser with the olive oil, lemon juice and seasonings until smooth, or mash with a fork. Fold in the whipped double cream, the mayonnaise (you can use Hellman's or Salarad) and the salmon. Divide into small pots and cover with a round of lemon to prevent the avocado discolouring. Chill and serve with hot toast or thinly sliced brown bread and butter.

Brown Bread Ice Cream

To make about 2 pints (1·14 litres/5⅛ cups) enough for 8–10 people
4 eggs, separated
4 oz (120 g/about 1¼ cups) sieved icing sugar
½ pint (0·28 litres/1¼ cups) double cream
1 cup brown breadcrumbs
½ cup Demerara sugar

Scatter the Demerara sugar over the breadcrumbs and caramelise them under the grill. Cool and crush them (the easiest way is to blend them at low speed in the liquidiser, till crushed but not pulverised). Whisk the egg whites until stiff, then whisk in the icing sugar 1 tablespoon at a time until stiff. Whisk in the egg yolks. Beat the cream until thick enough to hang on to the whisk and fold it into the meringue along with the crushed breadcrumbs. Put in a lidded container and freeze in the freezing compartment of your refrigerator. It can be served straight from the freezer and is absolutely delicious.

YAN ... TYAN ... TETHERA ... (A, B)

70 Main Street, Keswick
Tel: Keswick 72033
Open (Summer) 11 am to 3 pm; 6.30 pm to 10 pm
Closed Monday evening
(Winter) 11 am to 2.30 pm; 11 am to 5.30 pm at weekends

Three fun sheep and a name that sounds like the refrain from a nursery rhyme (it actually means 1, 2, 3 in Norse) decorate the façade of what used to be four of the oldest cottages in Keswick. Inside is a cheery welcome and sunshine colours – golds and yellow, light wood and local pottery. More often than not the fresh flowers on each table are the gift of customers who have become regulars and friends of the owner and presiding genius, Simone Boddington – Simone to all.

The cooking is done in the open-plan kitchen, enabling the staff to chat to customers. The food is simple and good and Simone, who devises most of the dishes, is a dab hand at finding short cuts with no loss in quality or flavour (see her recipe for Lemon Mayonnaise). She serves local specialities – Cumberland Sausage, Rum Butter and Lakeland Syllabub; always has fresh vegetables (unusual fillings for jacket potatoes) and her Shrimp Suppers (from May to October) are known by people all over the world. Giant South Sea shrimps cooked in olive oil and garlic and served with the mayonnaise, a piquante sauce and a fresh green salad. There are tea time treats using rum butter and home-made Cherry Pie and Apple Cheesecake and the prices are as refreshing, in these days of inflated costs, as the atmosphere.

RECIPES FROM YAN ... TYAN ... TETHERA

Lakeland Syllabub

For 6 people
  6 oz (180 g/1⅓ cups) caster sugar
  juice of 1 large lemon

a little ratafia essence
1½ pints (0·85 litres/4 cups) whipping cream
8 fl oz (2·27 decilitres/1 cup) dark rum

Place all the ingredients (except the cream) in the blender. When well blended, add the cream and blend at slow speed until all mixed. Serve in glasses accompanied by sponge fingers. If you have no blender, beat the sugar with the lemon juice, rum and ratafia essence until it's all combined then add the cream and beat until slightly thickened.

Simone's Strong Rum Butter

This, potted and sealed, will keep for three or four months.
3½ lb (1·680 kg/10 cups) dark Barbados sugar
1½ lb (720 g/3 cups) best butter
7 fl oz (just under 2·27 decilitres/just under 1 cup) dark rum
cinnamon and mixed spices to taste

Cream together in the mixer, slowly at first and then faster until well amalgamated. Pot and seal in clean jars. Simone serves her Rum Butter on scones, split and warmed under the grill with a little whipped cream.

Instant Lemon Mayonnaise

4 whole eggs
⅓ cup salt, sugar and dry mustard mixed in equal quantities
2 pints (1·14 litres/5⅓ cups) good quality oil – olive oil is best
½ cup PLJ pure lemon juice

Blend eggs, salt and sugar and mustard mixture together, then add the oil slowly and go on blending; finally add the lemon juice slowly. The sauce will keep in the refrigerator for 2–3 weeks. It's very good with all seafoods.

SHARROW BAY COUNTRY HOUSE HOTEL (C)

Lake Ullswater, Penrith, Cumbria
Tel: Pooley Bridge 301/483
Open 1 pm to 1.30 pm; 7.45 pm to 8.30 pm (Guests are all served at one sitting at lunch and dinner). Closed December and January

The Lake District, in Cumbria, offers some of England's finest scenery and one of our best hotels: Sharrow Bay, on the edge of Lake Ullswater. The building, which owes its Victorian looks to a front built on to the original two-hundred-year-old cottage in 1840, was privately owned until 1949. Then Francis Coulson bought it from two old ladies and, with £500 in the bank, a red setter called Peggy, and plenty of determination, set about the long job of creating a luxury home from home. Three years later, he was joined by his present partner, Brian Sack.

Over the years, the hotel has expanded and today guests can also be housed in an adjacent cottage in the twelve-acre grounds, or the Lodge four hundred yards away, or Thwaite Cottage four miles away at Tirril, or Bank House a mile along the Lake. But dinner for everyone is served in the main hotel – an ingenious feast of tempting dishes with generous portions, personally supervised by Francis and Brian. Along with a love of good food and an ability to make people feel at home, the proprietors have an instinct for collecting, so the reception rooms are full of interesting ornaments. Furnishings everywhere are rich and comfortable and the bedrooms – each one called by a Victorian name – are stocked with books, a portable radio, hair-dryer and 'Scrabble' for guests' entertainment.

As you would imagine, views from the rooms are superb, often looking across the wide lake to the spectacular peaks and fells. If – like many of the guests – you have come to explore this countryside, the hotel will provide you with a delicious picnic lunch. Just another of the thoughtful touches that puts Sharrow Bay into the top league of world-famous hotels.

RECIPES FROM SHARROW BAY

Brandy Angel Cream Mousse

For 6 people
  3 eggs, separated
  6 oz (180 g/1⅓ cups) caster sugar
  ½ oz (15 g/1½ tablespoons) gelatine
  ½ pint (0·28 litres/1⅓ cups) double cream
  1½ tablespoons brandy
  1½ tablespoons rum

Beat the egg yolks and the sugar until thick and creamy and forming a ribbon. Add the brandy and rum and continue beating. Dissolve the gelatine in a little water, add to the mixture and continue beating. In a separate bowl beat the cream until thick, then beat the egg whites until stiff. When the gelatine mixture has thickened, fold in the cream and lastly the egg whites. Pour into individual pots and chill in the refrigerator.

Stuffed Loin of English Lamb

The combination of cucumber, onion and mint makes a delicious fresh filling for this lamb dish.

For about 4 people
Have a loin of lamb boned; remove any surplus fat and sinews

The stuffing:
  ½ cucumber
  1 small onion
  1 beaten egg
  1 tablespoon finely chopped fresh mint
  fresh white breadcrumbs to make a stiff consistency

salt and freshly ground pepper
a little butter for cooking

Prepare the stuffing by peeling and de-seeding the cucumber; chop it up small, chop the onion and the mint very finely and sauté both with the cucumber in a little butter, do not overcook this. Mix in bread-crumbs and beaten egg, beat to a stiff consistency. Place down the centre of the loin of lamb. Roll and tie with string every 1½ inches (37mm). Roast at Gas Mark 5 (375°F/190°C) for 20 minutes per lb and 20 minutes over. Alternatively you can part roast the meat, roll it in puff pastry, let it stand for a little and bake at Gas Mark 4 until pastry is nicely browned. Serve with onion sauce and mint jelly.

NORTHUMBRIA

Cleveland, Durham, Northumberland, Tyne and Wear

WHITE SWAN HOTEL (A)

Bondgate Within, Alnwick, Northumberland
Tel: Alnwick 2109
Open 12 noon to 2 pm; 7 pm to 9 pm

Northumberland nudges the border regions of Scotland and you can still see some of the strong fortifications put up against surprise raids. At Alnwick, the Percy family (Dukes of Northumberland) built a magnificent Norman fortress to keep their lands safe. Part of this castle – the keep, armoury, library and other principal apartments with pictures by Titian, Canaletto and Van Dyck – is on view from May to September. The castle overlooks some of the rooms at the White Swan Hotel, once a staging post for horse-drawn coaches from London to Edinburgh and haunt of highwaymen, now fully modernised with forty bedrooms. In the restaurant at lunchtime, there is often a 'Taste of England' menu on offer (as well as the à la carte); this features such traditional dishes as Leek and Potato soup, Pork and Pease pudding, and Plum Bolster, and the very reasonable price includes your entrance fee to Alnwick or another of the local castles.

RECIPES FROM THE WHITE SWAN HOTEL

Liver and Onion Casserole

For 4 people
1 lb (480 g) lamb's liver
2 large onions
4 oz (120 g/1 cup) flour
4 oz (120 g/½ cup) of lard (or butter and oil)
1 pint (0·57 litres/2⅔ cups) of stock
salt and pepper

Melt the fat in a pan, dip the sliced liver in seasoned flour and fry gently. Add the sliced onion and fry until half cooked. Put in an oven-proof dish, add stock and cook in the oven at Gas Mark 4 (350°F/180°C) for 15–20 minutes. Served with creamed potatoes and a fresh green vegetable.

BOWES MOOR HOTEL (B)

Bowes Moor, Barnard Castle, Teesdale, County Durham
Tel: Bowes 331
Open breakfast till 9.30 am; 12 noon to 2 pm; 6.30 to 9.30 pm
(10 pm for Bar meals)

Bowes Moor is the highest hotel in England, standing 1,300 feet above sea level, surrounded by glorious, unspoilt moorland. Time seems to have stood still here as you wander among the acres of surrounding heather-clad moors, full of birds and other wild-life. Within a few yards of the hotel are the remains of signal stations built by the Romans; just down the road, the famous Pennine Way offers a hundred miles of walking to the intrepid, with the natural phenomenon of 'God's Bridge' – a stone arch washed into shape over the centuries by the river – on the way.

You are within easy reach of Scotland or the Lake District by car, but there is plenty to see of historic and scenic value right on the doorstep.

Mark and Joanne Johns, who own the Bowes Moor Hotel, have built up a well-deserved reputation for good food; one of their specialities is grouse, locally shot – see the recipe below. Meals are either served in the restaurant, or less formally in the attractive bar. Families are welcome to bring the children, and can take advantage of a special rate for a Family Room. All sorts of outdoor hobbies are catered for in the area, including golf, pony trekking, water ski-ing, sailing, rowing, fishing and shooting.

RECIPE FROM BOWES MOOR HOTEL

Casserole of Bowes Moor Grouse

For 4 people
4 grouse
12 shallots

1 stick celery
8 oz (240 g) mushrooms
4 oz (120 g/½ cup) butter
2–3 level dessertspoons plain flour
1 pint (0·57 litres/2⅔ cups) stock
thyme, marjoram and rosemary
salt and freshly-ground pepper
3–4 tablespoons double cream
a little lemon juice
4 large round slices of bread
1 dessertspoon chopped parsley
2 tablespoons brandy

Peel the shallots and leave whole. Scrub the celery, trim the mushrooms and chop both roughly. Melt half the butter in a flame-proof casserole and brown the trussed grouse and the shallots. Transfer the bird and shallots to a warm plate. Gently fry the celery and mushrooms until soft. Remove the casserole from the heat and stir in sufficient flour to absorb the fat. Return pan to heat. Cook flour and fat, stirring continuously until

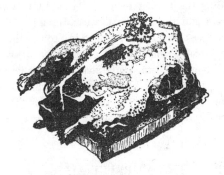

light golden in colour, then gradually blend in the stock. Bring the mixture to simmering point and season to taste with herbs, salt and pepper. Return the grouse and shallots to the casserole, cover with a lid and cook over low heat for 1½ hours. When grouse are tender, mix cream and brandy together, blend in 2 or 3 tablespoons of sauce from the casserole and stir back into dish. Sharpen the taste with a little lemon juice and adjust seasonings. Using a clean pan, fry the bread in the remaining butter until crisp and golden. Drain and arrange on a hot serving dish.

On each slice of bread place one grouse and over each grouse pour a little of the sauce and a sprinkling of parsley. Pour remaining sauce into a sauceboat. Serve with game chips and a tossed green salad.

THE MORRITT ARMS HOTEL (B)

Greta Bridge, Barnard Castle, County Durham
Tel: Whorlton 232
Open 8 am to 9.30 am; 12.30 pm to 2 pm; 7.30 pm to 9 pm

If you turn your back upon the A1 at Scotch Corner and head west towards the Lake District, within ten miles you will come to the Morritt Arms. It's a sprawling yellow Yorkshire sandstone building, creeper-clad and set well back from the A66, with its own views of the River Greta and the edge of the Yorkshire Dales. All year the crackle of open log fires greets you and there are always bowls of fresh flowers on polished wood tables in the two bars and the sitting room. It's a perfect jumping-off point for touring the beauty spots of Teesdale, High Force, Cauldron Snout and the Lake District. But there is also plenty to see locally, including the market town of Barnard Castle with a twelfth-century fortress and the famous Bowes Museum. And – one mile's walk away – Egglestone Abbey, founded in 1190 by the White Canons. The Morritt Arms is run on very personal lines by owner Rodney Waldron and his wife, Clare. Daily menus are simple but imaginative using best quality ingredients with lots of local fresh foods. Here is their recipe for Jugged Hare, one of their regular 'Taste of England' dishes, and for Cherry Pie, which you can see on the cover of this book.

RECIPES FROM THE MORRITT ARMS

Jugged Hare

For 4–6 people
   1 hare
   2 large onions
   2 large carrots
   ¼ lb (120 g) bacon trimmings
   ½ bottle red wine

1 small glass of port
2 bay leaves
pinch of thyme
6 black peppercorns
a little flour
salt and freshly-ground black pepper
1 tablespoon olive oil
fat for frying
2 pints (1·14 litres/5¼ cups) beef stock
1 tablespoon tomato purée
4 slices of bread
a little chopped parsley
a little redcurrant jelly

Skin the hare and cut into 12 pieces, retaining the blood in a bowl. Marinade the meat in the red wine, olive oil, sliced onions and carrots, herbs and bacon trimmings for 24 hours, turning frequently. Remove the meat from the marinade, flour lightly and shallow fry in hot fat, turning once. Place in a casserole and keep warm. Drain off vegetables from the marinade, and keep the liquid. Fry off the vegetables and add sufficient flour to absorb the fat. Add the tomato purée and the stock and bring to the boil. Skim and add to hare with the liquid from the marinade. Cook in the oven at Gas Mark 7 (425°F/220°C) for 2–3 hours, until hare is tender. Transfer hare into a clean pan and strain the sauce over it, add the blood and port, correct the seasoning and serve immediately garnished with croutons of bread, shallow fried and dipped in redcurrant jelly and parsley. Serve redcurrant jelly separately.

Cherry Pie

For 6–8 people

The pastry:
10 oz (300 g/2½ cups) plain flour

2 oz (60 g/½ cup) cornflour
6 oz (180 g/¾ cup) butter
1 oz (30 g/⅛ cup) sugar
ice cold water to mix

The filling:
1 lb (480 g) fresh cherries
2 oz (60 g/just under ½ cup) caster sugar
1 oz (30 g/2 tablespoons) melted butter
1 oz (30 g/just under ¼ cup) fine tapioca
a couple of drops almond essence

Stone the cherries and cook them in a sugar syrup. Drain them and mix well with rest of filling ingredients. Make the pastry by working the butter into the dry ingredients, mix to a paste with the water and roll out. Line a pie plate with the pastry, put on the cherry mixture and cover the plate with the rest of the pastry. Bake in the oven at Gas Mark 6 (400°F/200°C) for 30–40 minutes. Serve hot with cream. If you prefer, make the pie as in our cover photograph, with just a pastry lid. In this case, make only half the amount of pastry, put the cherry mixture in a pie dish and cover with pastry, decorate and bake as already described.

THE MILECASTLE INN (A, B)

Military Road, Haltwhistle, Northumberland
Tel: Haltwhistle 682
Open 11.30 am to 2.30 pm; 6.30 pm to 10.15 pm

The Milecastle Inn stands only five hundred yards from the famous stone wall that Hadrian built across the country to save England from invasion by the Scots, and was built with the same stone, though not until the late seventeenth century. Another distinguishing feature of the Milecastle is that it is the only inn in England to hold a game dealer's licence. You would be right if you guessed from this that the speciality of the house is game – locally shot, often cooked with wine, and served with fresh vegetables. Chef *patrons* Jenny and Barrie Smith also smoke their own hams and fish; and pâtés, sauces and bread are made on the premises. In the mornings, from 11 am to 12.30 pm, you can have an 'English breakfast grill' of home-cured, oak-smoked bacon, lambs' kidneys, home-made pork sausages, free-range eggs, tomatoes, potatoes and coffee. But whatever time of day you want to eat in this small privately-owned restaurant, you must book to be sure of getting one of only twenty-eight seats.

RECIPE FROM THE MILECASTLE INN

Partridge Roasted in Madeira

1 partridge per person
fat smoked bacon
2 bay leaves
Madeira wine
lemon zest
1 clove garlic
black pepper
rosemary
nutmeg
cognac

If you have a larding needle, cut the bacon into ¼-inch thick strips, about 1½ inches long, and with the needle sew them into the partridge's breast. Otherwise simply lay strips of fat bacon on the bird's breast when you roast it. Make a marinade of the Madeira wine, the bay leaves, a crushed clove of garlic, a pinch of rosemary and nutmeg, a little lemon zest and black pepper. Lay the birds breast down in it and leave them for 48 hours. Then put the birds in the marinade in a moderate oven, Gas Mark 4 (350°F/180°C) and cook for about an hour. When the birds are tender, put them on a serving dish to keep warm. Strain the marinade and reduce it over a high heat adding a little cognac just before serving.

JIM AND CAROLE'S KITCHEN (A, C)

89–91 Blenheim St, Newcastle-upon-Tyne
Tel: Newcastle-upon-Tyne 24660
Open 12 noon to 3 pm; 7.30 pm to 1 am
Closed Sunday and Saturday lunch

Jim and Carole are husband and wife, and their 'kitchen' is a restaurant in what used to be three terraced houses now knocked into one in the old part of Newcastle. Jim has been in catering since 1959, when he started work with the P & O luxury liner *Arcadia*; this is his third restaurant in the city, though it is the first with Carole. They opened in 1976, with a view to 'providing traditional English fare', which has proved very popular with customers. Carole supervises the restaurant while Jim cooks and presents all the food.

On the dinner menu, we noticed such delicacies as Seagulls eggs in Tartare sauce, along with the more traditional Devilled Kidneys, among the starters. In season you'll find Pheasant in wine and cream, and Venison chops, char grilled, with barbecue sauce as well as other game dishes, fish, beef and steaks, for main courses, with a selection of sweets or cheese to follow.

RECIPE FROM JIM AND CAROLE'S KITCHEN

Devilled Kidneys

This, usually served as a savoury, can also make a good starter.

For 4 people
12 oz (360 g) lamb's kidneys cut in half
2 glasses port wine
1 cup gravy
½ cup fresh cream
freshly ground black pepper
salt
a little oil and butter for cooking
chives for garnish
4 slices of toast

Sauté the kidneys in the oil and butter, season with a sprinkle of salt and a generous amount of pepper. Add the port wine and the gravy together with the cream. Cook until the kidneys are done and the sauce has thickened – about 15–20 minutes. Serve on slices of hot toast, sprinkled with chives.

NORTH WEST

Cheshire, Greater Manchester, Lancashire, Merseyside

HARROP FOLD FARM GUEST HOUSE (B)

Harrop Fold, Bolton-by-Bowland, Lancashire
Tel: Bolton-by-Bowland 600

Open from February 1 to November 30 to residents only for breakfast, tea and high tea (4.30 pm to 6.30 pm); dinner (8 pm)

As well as a guest house, Harrop Fold is essentially a working farm, all 288 acres of it. Peter and Victoria Wood have forty cows and two hundred sheep, which Peter copes with virtually single-handed, helped out by his family when necessary. Victoria always wanted to be a farmer's wife and loves cooking and presenting food, so she finds life on the farm and taking in guests 'my ideal'.

The Woods started the accommodation side in 1970, with two guest rooms, but word soon spread and they had so many applications that now they have given up the whole of their seventeenth-century farmhouse and a new wing to visitors, and moved themselves and their three children into an adjoining building which was once stabling.

Guests tell Victoria in the morning if they will be in for dinner that night. There is no set menu, Victoria (who does all the cooking) likes to vary meals and make them as interesting as possible. In summer, Wednesday night is Lancashire night, with Brawn, Black Pudding, Tripe and Onions, Morecambe Bay Shrimp Puffs, and other regional specialities. In autumn and winter, Victoria lays on an Old English Game Buffet every Saturday evening, with a tremendous selection of local game, followed by syllabub, trifle, cheesecake and cheeses.

RECIPE FROM HARROP FOLD FARM

Ribble Valley Chicken Casserole

For 6 people
I fresh chicken
I onion
I bay leaf
salt and pepper
sprig parsley
I carrot
small piece celery

The sauce:
I onion
1½–2 oz (45–60 g/3–4 tablespoons) butter
1½–2 oz (45–60 g/⅓–½ cup flour)
I onion
½ pint (0·28 litres/1¼ cups) milk or half milk, half stock
½ gill (0·75 decilitres/⅓ cup) vermouth
salt and freshly ground black pepper
½ green pepper, de-seeded and diced
I small apple, peeled, cored and sliced
pinch of thyme
chopped parsley
a little garlic salt

2 or 3 teaspoons tomato purée
¼ lb (120 g) mushrooms

Cook the chicken in water with the onion, carrot, celery, bay leaf, parsley and salt and pepper, until *just* cooked. Leave to cool and then joint and put in an oven-proof casserole. Make the sauce. Poach the onion in the milk with a little butter until soft. Make a roux with the rest of the butter and flour, add milk or milk-and-stock; add the vermouth, salt and pepper, garlic salt, parsley and thyme, then the tomato purée, the diced pepper and the apples. Cook for a few minutes then pour the sauce over the chicken in the casserole. Slice the mushrooms and place over the chicken pieces. Cover casserole and cook in the oven at Gas Mark 3–4 (325–350°F/160–180°C) for about ¾ hour until thoroughly cooked through.

TRUFFLES (B, C)

63 Bridge Street, Manchester 3
Tel: 061 832 9393
Open for lunch on Wednesday and Thursday: 12.00 pm to 2 pm
(last orders); Sunday: 1 pm to 2.30 pm (last orders)
Open for dinner Tuesday, Wednesday, Thursday, Friday,
Saturday: 7 pm to 12.30 am (last orders)
Closed on Sunday night and Monday

You walk upstairs to the bar at Truffles – except that there is no bar! The drinks are laid out on a table, as they would be at home, there's an open log fire, dark green walls, pretty fabrics, candlelight – everything in fact to relax customers and make them feel at home. Not that many homes provide food as good and imaginative as Truffles! Most of the recipes have been adapted by Rikki Hedley Charlton, who started Truffles and runs it with great verve, from old English recipe books.

In the restaurant downstairs – the same green walls, flowered curtains, soft lights and flowers and plants – you might see a famous actor, visiting film stars, members of the Royal Ballet: everybody who is anybody goes to Truffles. 'People actually come into Manchester to eat,' says Rikki.

The menu changes every month – we looked at a mind-boggling year's selection with things like Smoked Salmon Barbara (stuffed with chopped eggs, tomato and mayonnaise), Chilled Strawberry and Mint Soup with

Sour Cream, Melon Mahogany (Melon balls soaked in gin and black treacle) and chose the three delicious recipes below for you. The lovely hot Carrot Pudding (brought over by the English from India in the late nineteenth century), Vectis Onions stuffed with lambs' kidneys (Vectis is the old name for the Isle of Wight) and an unusual sauce for grilled steak.

RECIPES FROM TRUFFLES

Carrot Pudding

For 3–4 people
¾ lb (360 g) large carrots
4 cups buttermilk or ordinary milk
1 cup double cream
¾ cup white sugar
1 tablespoon of sultanas (or more, to taste)
2 oz (60 g/4 tablespoons) butter
pinch of saffron, soaked in the cream for 1 hour

Grate the carrots on a thickish grater. Bring the milk to the boil in a heavy-bottomed large saucepan, add the cream, saffron and carrots. Cook over low heat for about two hours until all the milk and cream have been absorbed (stirring all the time if possible). Add the sultanas, butter and sugar and mix thoroughly. Keep on simmering and allow to dry out as much as possible. Serve it hot or cold with lots of cream.

Vectis Onions

For 4 people
8 large onions
8 lamb's kidneys
home-made onion gravy
pinch of mixed herbs
salt and freshly ground black pepper

Part bake the onions in a medium oven, Gas Mark 4 (350°F/180°C) for 1 hour with their skins on. Then remove the skins and take out enough of the centre to accommodate one kidney. Sprinkle on the herbs, pepper and salt. Using the same baking tray, cook for another 35 minutes at the same temperature. Remove stuffed onions to a hot dish and use the residue in the tray to make gravy. Serve with lots of gravy.

Charlton's Sauce

Good with beef, particularly with grilled steak.

> *1 lb (480 g) fresh blackberries*
> *¼ lb (120 g/½ cup) butter*
> *2 large chopped onions*
> *1 dessertspoon beef bouillon*
> *salt and freshly ground pepper*

Cook the chopped onions in half the butter until golden, add the blackberries and rest of butter with the bouillon and crush berries with wooden spoon, continue until cooked. Add a little water if too thick, season and pour on hot grilled meat.

CHURCHE'S MANSION (A, B)

Hospital Street, Nantwich, Cheshire
Tel: Nantwich 65933
Open 12 noon to 2 pm; 7 pm to 8.30 pm
Closed Sunday night

If you get involved with a beautiful old house – beware! Before you know what's happening, you may have been taken over, which is what happened to the Myott family in the case of Churche's Mansion. This Tudor House was allowed to fall derelict by descendants of the rich merchant, Richard Churche, who built it in Elizabeth I's reign. In 1930, its beautiful bones almost hidden by later additions over the centuries, it stood desolate and dark and no one wanted to buy it. Then a middle-aged doctor, Edgar Myott, and his wife became 'intrigued with its possibilities'. Alarmed to hear that it had been advertised for sale in America, they determined by hook or by crook to raise the money to outbid the American syndicate, and to restore the house to its original state. How they did this, and how their son, Richard, and his wife took up where they left off is very well told in the guide book to the house.

To offset the steep running costs of keeping this fine half-timbered house in a state of preservation, the Myotts run a licensed restaurant on the ground floor. As you would expect, the food is English, with several seasonal specialities each day (and Real Ale, straight from the barrel).

RECIPES FROM CHURCHE'S MANSION

Casserole of Pigeon

For 6 people
6 pigeons
1 sliced onion
10–12 sliced mushrooms
3 oranges
¼ pint (0·28 litres/1¼ cups) red wine
½ pint (0·28 litres/1¼ cups) stock
6 slices streaky bacon
bouquet garni
salt and pepper
2 oz (60 g/4 tablespoons) butter
1–1½ oz (30–45 g/¼–⅓ cup) flour

Peel the oranges, cut in half and stuff each bird. Wrap each bird in a slice
of bacon and fry in the butter until brown. Place in a casserole. Fry the
mushrooms and onions; stir in sufficient flour to make a roux. Blend
in the red wine and the stock, season to taste and add the bouquet garni.

Cook in a moderate oven – Gas Mark 3 (325°F/160°C) until tender – about 1½–2 hours.

Curried Chicken Mousse

For 6 people
8 oz (240 g) cooked chicken
1 dessertspoon curry powder
2 oz (60 g/4 tablespoons) butter
2 oz (60 g/½ cup) flour
½ pint (0·28 litres/1¼ cups) stock
¼ pint (1·5 decilitres/⅔ cup) sherry
2 egg whites
1 oz (30 g/2½ tablespoons) powdered gelatine
¼ pint (1·5 decilitres/⅔ cup) cream
1 onion, finely chopped

Fry the onion in the butter until soft, add the curry powder and fry a little longer. Add the flour, then blend in the stock to make a thick sauce. Steep the gelatine in the sherry and dissolve over hot water. Add to the sauce. When cool, add the cream. Mince the cold chicken and add to the other ingredients. Whip the egg whites until stiff and fold in. Pour into a mould and leave to set. Turn out and serve with a green salad and a rice or potato salad as a main course or on lettuce with hot buttered toast as a starter.

WATERSIDE RESTAURANT (A, B)

166 Stockport Road, Romiley, Stockport
Tel: 061 430 4302 and 427 2420
Open 12 noon to 2 pm; 7 pm to 9.30 pm
Closed on Mondays

Monty Small, who is the owner of Waterside Restaurant and does the cooking, is a Master Craftsman of the Guild of Chefs. The food, with such traditional English fare as Elizabethan Rabbit, Lancashire Steak Pie and Beef Cobbler, lives up to his qualifications and is excellent value for money. The restaurant is a family concern (his son David is a sommelier, and also a trained chef), housed in a two hundred-year-old cottage which backs on to the Peak Forest canal, hence its name. Inside, the original beams were retained when the cottage was converted for use as a restaurant in the 1960s, and when you dine here by candlelight you can enjoy a pleasant feeling of going back into the past. Book before going, since there is room for thirty-six people only.

RECIPE FROM WATERSIDE RESTAURANT

Tipsy Hedgehog

A delicious no-cook pudding that is quick and easy to make.

For 6–8 people
1 1lb (480 g) packet digestive biscuits
½ lb (240 g) plain dark chocolate
1 or 2 glasses of sweet red wine (we used cherry wine)
½ pint (0·28 litres/1¼ cups) whipping cream

Line a 7-inch bread tin with foil on the base and along the two long sides and half fill with the roughly broken biscuits. Grate ¾ of the chocolate on top and cover with the rest of the broken biscuits, pour on enough of the wine to really moisten the biscuits, cover and leave for at least 12 hours. Then take it out by pulling on the foil and put it on the serving dish. With your hands mould it into a hedgehog shape, whip the cream and cover the hedgehog with it. Grate the rest of the chocolate over it and serve it slightly chilled.

THE RIVER HOUSE (B, C)

Skippool Creek, Thornton-le-Fylde, Lancashire
Open lunch 1 pm, dinner 7.30 pm
Closed on Mondays, also 1 week February, 2 weeks August, Xmas and Boxing Day, May Day and Summer Bank Holiday Monday.

The River House has had an excellent reputation for food and lodging for over twenty years, so you must ring in advance to make certain of your place. Jean Scott, with her son Bill and his wife Jed, take a lot of trouble to make their guests' rooms seem like home, and each one is named instead of numbered, and stocked with home-made biscuits in case you get hungry in the night. The standard of cooking is consistently high, and Jean Scott believes in fresh foods in season freshly cooked. Regional specialities are frequently on the menu.

Home-made Sausages (Skinless)

For 4 people
¼ lb (240 g) belly of pork
½ lb (240 g) pie veal or braising steak
¼ lb (120 g/2 cups) granary breadcrumbs
grated rind of ¼ lemon
pinch each of thyme, savory and marjoram
¼ teaspoonful each of grated nutmeg and sage
salt and freshly ground black pepper
1 or 2 egg yolks to bind
a little flour
oil or fat for frying

Get your butcher to mince the pork with the veal or braising steak. To this mixture add the breadcrumbs, the lemon rind and all the herbs and seasonings. Add enough egg yolk to bind, form into sausages, roll in flour and fry for about 10 minutes. You can also dip the sausages in coating batter and deep fry.

Old English Orange Boodles

For 4–5 people
6 sponge cakes cut into cubes
¼ pint (1·5 decilitres/⅔ cup) orange juice
½ pint (0·28 litres/1¼ cups) double cream
1 whole orange cut into slices or segments

Cut the sponge cakes into cubes, soak in the orange juice for about an hour, toss gently and serve in a glass dish covered with the whipped cream and decorated with orange slices or segments.

THE INN AT WHITEWELL (A, B)

Whitewell, Forest of Bowland, near Clitheroe, Lancashire
Tel: Dunsop Bridge 222
Open 12 noon to 2 pm; 7 pm to 9.30 pm (residents only on
Monday and Tuesday evening)

Getting away from it all is no problem if you head for the Inn at Whitewell, in the Forest of Bowland. Here you can enjoy five hundred acres of rough shooting, climbing the Fells and five miles of excellent salmon and trout fishing on the river Hodder. (In fact, the Inn is on the banks of the Hodder.) If you like walking, the countryside is lovely and unspoilt in this part of Lancashire and facilities for riding and playing golf are close at hand. Apart from the hotel, Whitewell village consists of the church, three cottages and a farm, so you are not likely to be bothered by noise from neighbours!

The Inn was renovated recently – not to change the period feeling of the house, which dates back to the fourteenth century in places, but to refurnish it with antiques.

Robert and Lesley Orr, who run the Inn, are Cordon Bleu cooks with practical experience, and Lesley taught for some time at Winkfield and Leith's cookery schools. As well as dinner most evenings, the hotel is open for bar lunches every day, with home-made soup, pâté, steak and kidney pie, and quiches; and for tea, with home-made cakes and biscuits.

RECIPES FROM THE INN AT WHITEWELL

Watercress and Onion Flan

For 4–6 people
This makes a good main course for lunch accompanied by a tomato salad, or, served in smaller portions, an unusual starter.

The pastry:
8 oz (240 g/2 cups) plain flour
6 oz (180 g/¾ cup) butter
pinch of salt
1 beaten egg
about 1 tablespoon water

The filling:
1 large bunch watercress
2 small onions
2 oz (60 g/4 tablespoons) butter
2 whole eggs and 1 egg yolk
¼ pint (1·5 decilitres/⅔ cup) milk

36

¼ pint (1·5 decilitres/⅔ cup) double cream
salt and freshly ground pepper

Make the pastry by rubbing the butter into the sifted flour and salt. Bind with the egg and water, roll out and line a flan tin. Bake it 'blind' for about 15 minutes at Gas Mark 5 (375°F/190°C). In the meantime make the filling by slicing the onions finely and softening them in the butter. When partly cooked, add the washed and coarsely chopped watercress (stalks and leaves). Cook for a further 3–4 minutes. Season with salt and pepper. Put the onion and watercress mixture in the bottom of the partly cooked flan, pour on the cream, milk and eggs which have been beaten together with salt and pepper. Bake in the oven at Gas Mark 5 (375°F/190°C) for 20–30 minutes, until filling is set, and slightly brown on top.

Pancakes Stuffed with Spinach

For 4–6 people
The pancake batter:
  ½ pint (0·28 litres/1¼ cups) milk
  4 oz (120 g/1 cup) plain flour
  1 whole egg and 1 egg yolk
  1 tablespoon oil
  pinch of salt

The filling:
  1–1½ lb (480–720 g) fresh spinach, cooked and roughly chopped
  6–8 oz (180–240 g) cream cheese
  pinch nutmeg
  2 tablespoons of cream
  a little grated cheese to finish

Put all the ingredients for the pancake batter into a liquidiser and blend for 20 seconds. Or beat together by hand, mixing the eggs and half the milk into the flour gradually, beating for 4 or 5 minutes then adding the rest of the milk and the oil. Leave batter to stand for half an hour. While mixture is resting make the filling. Beat the cream cheese with the cream; when soft beat in the chopped spinach. Add a large pinch of nutmeg, salt and pepper to taste. Fry the pancakes. Lay out the pancakes, put a little stuffing on each, fold them in half and place in a dish or baking tray. Sprinkle liberally with grated cheese and brown under the grill or in a hot oven.

THE LIVELY LOBSTER (C)

The Quay, Peel, Isle of Man
Tel: Peel 2789
Open 12.30 pm to 2.30 pm (last orders); 7.30 pm to 10 pm (last
orders)
Closed October to February

Perhaps the Isle of Man's best known export is the delicious kipper.
Plump and succulent, its colour and flavour comes entirely from the
smoking as Manx law forbids the use of dyes. There is also local cheese
and very good ice cream.

The island has its own Parliament, the ancient House of Keys; its
own very favourable rate of income tax and a breed of tail-less cats,
found nowhere else! It's an interesting place for a holiday, offering a
rich variety of scenery in a relatively small area, from the tourist attractions of Douglas to small unspoilt bays, sleepy villages where it's easy
to believe the local legends about witches and Little People, and a
mountain with its own railway.

On the quayside in the charming old city of Peel you will find the
Lively Lobster, whose very good fish mainly comes straight from the
fishing vessels landing literally a few feet away. Customers are encouraged to choose from the lobsters, crabs, soles, plaice, salmon,
prawns and scallops on display. A la carte meals are available but the
best value is offered by the set menu of five courses and coffee.

A family concern, the Lively Lobster really lives up to its name in the
evenings, when guests are encouraged to play the pianola and join in the
odd sea shanty.

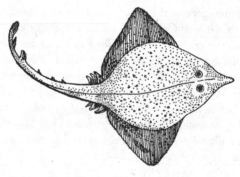

Scallops à la Peel

For 4 people
   16 good-sized fresh scallops
   1½–2 oz (45–60 g/3–4 tablespoons) butter
   1½–2 oz (45–60 g/⅓–½ cup) flour
   ½ pint (0·28 litres/1⅓ cups) milk or half milk, half single cream
   salt and pepper
   1 onion, thinly sliced
   ¼ gill (0·75 decilitres/⅓ cup) white wine
   a little paprika
   chopped parsley

Clean the scallops and remove the beards but not the tongues. Cut scallops into mouth-sized bites and set aside. Soften the onion in the butter and make a roux with it and the flour. Thin with the milk or half milk/half cream, add the wine and salt and pepper. Drop in the scallops and stir rapidly for 2–3 minutes. Turn out onto hot shells and dust with paprika and chopped parsley.

Skate on the Wing

Not many people are aware that skate should not be eaten fresh, but should be left to hang for 24 hours at least to get rid of the strong smell of ammonia which the fish has at certain times of the year. The wing should be skinned on both sides – as this is a rather tricky operation ask your fishmonger to do it for you – also check whether he has hung the skate.

For 1 person
   A 4–6 oz piece of skate wing
   1 onion, chopped
   2 oz (60 g/4 tablespoons) butter
   2 good tablespoons double cream
   1 bay leaf
   salt and pepper
   ¼ lemon

Soften the onion in the butter, add the cream and put in the skate with the salt and pepper and bay leaf. Cover and simmer gently for about 5 minutes, turn and cook the other side for 2 or 3 minutes until all translucency has disappeared. Serve with a wedge of lemon.

YORKSHIRE AND HUMBERSIDE

North, South and West Yorkshire, Humberside

THE POST HOUSE HOTEL (B)

Otley Road, Bramhope, Leeds, West Yorkshire
Crowther Restaurant open 12.30 pm to 2.30 pm; 7.30 pm to
10.30 pm
Closed Monday lunch, Sunday evening

The Post House at Bramhope is well placed for business travellers to the busy centres of Leeds, Bradford and Harrogate. But if you are bent on lighter pursuits – perhaps looking at the glorious ruins of Fountains Abbey, visiting the Brontë Parsonage Museum at Haworth, climbing from Wensleydale to Swaledale past the frightening 'Buttertubs' (deep holes in the granite rocks) or sampling the spirits of the highest pub in Britain – Tan Hill, where whisky is supposed to freeze in winter – then you are also well placed.

The Post House was built in 1971 and offers every modern convenience, with the accent on family comfort. Many of the bedrooms are designed for families with two children, at economic rates, and the Shuttle Buttery serves food all day long, with a special children's menu. The main restaurant – the Crowther – prides itself on its Gastronomic evenings, which have proved very popular. The daily menus offer a wide selection, which includes a 'Taste of England' meal and traditional lunch on Sundays, in addition to the regular extensive à la carte.

RECIPE FROM THE POST HOUSE HOTEL

Traditional Leek and Lamb Pudding

For 6 people

The filling:
  1½ lb (720 g) diced lean lamb
  1 lb (480 g) shredded leeks

2 oz (60 g) diced onions
4 oz (120 g) diced carrots
1 or 2 tablespoons tomato purée
1 pint (0·57 litres/2⅔ cups) brown stock
1 oz (30 g/2 tablespoons) dripping
½ bayleaf
pinch chopped parsley
salt and pepper to taste
2 oz (60 g/¼ cup) flour

The suet crust pastry:
¾ lb (360 g/3 cups) self-raising flour
¼ teaspoon salt
4½ oz (135 g) suet
just over ¼ pint (1·5 decilitres/⅔ cup) cold water to mix

Heat dripping in pan; add lamb, leeks, onion and carrots. Cook for 10 minutes, turning the lamb to seal it on all sides. Add flour and tomato purée and mix well; cook for a further 10 minutes, stirring often. Add stock and bay leaf, and bring to the boil. Cook for 40 minutes, then add in chopped parsley and seasoning.

To make suet crust pastry:
Mix flour and salt, stir in suet and mix to a soft dough, with cold water, making sure not to get it sticky. Roll out ⅔ of the mixture to line 6 individual pie dishes. Fill dishes with meat mixture; roll out remaining suet crust for lids, damp edges and press into position. Wrap in foil and steam for 40 minutes. Remove foil, clean up dishes before serving.

THE CLOSE HOUSE (B)

Giggleswick, Settle, North Yorkshire
Tel: Settle 3540
Open Easter to September for bed and breakfast; dinners by arrangement for residents only. Booking in advance essential.

'Our visitors come back and back!' says Bessie Hargreaves, joint proprietor with her husband of the Close House. It's the best testimony we know, and a visit to this peaceful seventeenth-century farmhouse at the end of a tree-lined drive soon shows you why. If you are looking for relaxation in lovely countryside, the Close House, surrounded by lilacs, laburnum, cherry and fir trees, with only four guest-rooms, is an excellent answer. Bessie does the cooking herself, and has a long-standing reputation for really good, home-made food. The day for residents begins with a hearty old-fashioned English breakfast of fruit juice, porridge and cream (or cereals or fruit), and bacon, sausage, egg and tomato . . . and ends with a 'Taste of England' dinner. There's a choice of four starters, followed by the traditional roast – beef, duckling, or lamb, and so on – with fresh vegetables; then a selection of tempting puddings, and local cheese.

It's not surprising that you have to book well in advance to beat the queue.

RECIPES FROM THE CLOSE HOUSE

Duck Soup

For 6–8 people

The stock:
> *1 duck carcass*
> *1 onion stuck with a couple of cloves*
> *1 stick of celery and the celery tops*
> *2 carrots*
> *1 leek*
> *1 bay leaf*
> *small bunch of parsley*

Place all the ingredients in a saucepan, just cover with water and simmer gently for about 3 hours.

The soup:
> *2 oz (60 g/4 tablespoons) butter*
> *1 tablespoon flour*
> *2 carrots, grated or sliced thinly*
> *1 stick of celery, chopped small*
> *1 onion, chopped small*
> *salt and freshly milled black pepper*

Melt the butter in a large saucepan, add the chopped vegetables, stir well then leave with the lid on for a quarter of an hour on a very, very low heat. Sprinkle on the flour, stir and add the strained duck stock, stirring all the time. Bring to simmering point then cook gently for half an hour. Check seasoning. Before serving put a swirl of cream and a little chopped parsley on top of each soup bowl.

Port and Prune Fool

For 4 people
4 oz (120 g) prunes
a little lemon rind
a cupful of ruby port
¼ pint (1·5 decilitres/⅔ cup) double cream
tablespoon of sugar, or to taste

Soak the prunes overnight. Simmer until tender in just enough water to cover, with the lemon rind and the sugar. Cool and remove the stones, put the stoned prunes, four tablespoonsful of the cooking syrup and the port into blender and blend till fairly smooth. Whip the cream, fold in the prune mixture and put into stemmed glasses to chill. Serve with more cream and boudoir biscuits.

MALLYAN SPOUT HOTEL (B)

Goathland, Whitby, North Yorkshire
Tel: Goathland 206
Open lunchtime bar snacks; 7 pm to 9 pm; Sunday lunch
12 noon to 1.45 pm

Mallyan Spout Hotel takes its name from a seventy-foot high waterfall that's near enough to walk to. This is just one of many attractions (including fishing, walking, golf, pony-trekking) for visitors to the ivy-clad stone hotel, in a beautiful setting of moorland and dales. And – steam fanatics take note – eighteen miles of historic track have been reopened near here to steam engines that whistle you through Goathland and the picturesque Newtondale Valley.

The hotel is under the management of Peter and Judy Heslop, who take care to see that the food lives up to the Mallyan Spout's high standards in other areas. Home-made soups and sweets, fresh vegetables, Yorkshire-fed meat and fresh fish (Peter or Judy buys this on the quay in Whitby) are on the daily menus. And if you are staying and have a

fancy for a particular dish not shown, the chances are that the chef will
produce it during your visit.

RECIPES FROM MALLYAN SPOUT HOTEL

Casserole of Lamb with Rosemary

For 4 people
1½ lb (720 g) middle neck of lamb
2 lb (960 g) of mixed vegetables – carrots, swede, turnip, celery,
    potatoes and onions
rosemary
salt and freshly ground black pepper
stock to cover

Prepare the vegetables, peel them and cut them into rings. Put them in
a fire-proof casserole, put the meat over them, season and add rosemary.
Cover with stock and cook in a slow oven, Gas Mark 3 (325°F/160°C)
for 3–4 hours, until meat is tender.

Granny Pierson's Rum and Ginger Surprise

For 4 people
12 ginger biscuits
4 oz (120 g/½ cup) unsalted butter
2 oz (60 g/⅓ cup) ground almonds
1–2 oz (30–60 g/¼–½ cup) icing sugar
4 oz (120 g/⅔ cup) raisins
a little rum
whipped cream for decorating

Soak the raisins in the rum for several hours. Beat the butter, almonds
and icing sugar together, then, allowing 3 biscuits per serving, spread
each biscuit with the almond butter, sprinkle with raisins and put in
layers in individual ramekins. Leave for 24 hours in a cold place.
Decorate with whipped cream and a few raisins.

THE BLACK SWAN HOTEL (A, B)

Market Place, Helmsley, North Yorkshire
Tel: Helmsley 466
Open 12.30 pm to 2.15 pm; 7 pm to 9.30 pm

In the heart of the ancient town of Helmsley is the Black Swan, overlooking the Market Place. The oldest part of the hotel dates back over four hundred years and has thick stone walls, adze-dressed oak timbers, a stone Tudor doorway (from the town's twelfth-century castle, now in ruins) and fine Jacobean panelling. Next comes a graceful Georgian house, which was taken over by the Black Swan in 1947 and, next to that, a black and white timber framed house which used to be the Vicarage until it, too, became part of the hotel.

Helmsley is a good touring centre: it's on the edge of 200,000 acres of glorious, wild moors, within easy access of the sea, and only twenty-four miles from York. Nearer still are the magnificent bones of Rievaulx Abbey (three miles distance) founded by the Cistercians in 1131; another Cistercian monastery – Byland Abbey – seven miles away; and Gilling Castle, five miles away.

Yorkshire offers gastronomic treats, too, and Mr and Mrs Hopper, who manage the Black Swan, play an active part in keeping regional dishes alive. Their table d'hôte at lunchtime and in the evenings regularly offers traditional fare, and adventurous breakfast-eaters can try such choice dishes as Black Pudding, Kedgeree and Kidneys on Toast before setting out on a day's exploring.

RECIPES FROM THE BLACK SWAN

Stilton, Celery and Walnut Fritters

For 4 people
4 oz (120 g) Stilton cheese
1 large stick celery
½ oz (15 g/about 2 tablespoons) finely chopped walnuts
1 egg
salt and freshly milled black pepper
a little flour for coating
fresh breadcrumbs for coating

oil for deep frying
lemon and parsley for garnishing

Grate the cheese and pass it through a sieve to purée it, add to it the finely chopped celery and walnuts. Use a little beaten egg if necessary to moisten the mixture to a suitable consistency for rolling. Check for seasoning and add pepper and a pinch of herbs or fresh parsley. With floured hands, shape into small balls and chill. When ready to cook dip in flour, egg and fresh breadcrumbs and deep fry for about 3–4 minutes until golden brown. Garnish with lemon and parsley and serve with pickle or chutney.

Yorkshire Hot-Pot

For 4 people
  8 rashers smoked bacon
  1 lb (480 g) of black pudding
  4 large potatoes
  2 onions
  stock to cover
  salt and freshly ground pepper
  pinch of mixed herbs

Lightly grill the bacon and cut it into small pieces. Peel, slice and par-boil the potatoes. Chop the onions. Layer the bacon, onion and black pudding in an earthenware dish with a sprinkling of seasonings and herbs in between each layer. Cover with stock and top with overlapping slices of potato. Brush with dripping and bake in a hot oven, Gas Mark 7 (420°F/220°C) for about 30 minutes.

Pan Fried Chicken in Oatmeal with Barley Wine Sauce

For 4 people
  4 chicken breasts
  flour for coating
  beaten egg for coating
  oatmeal for coating
  salt and freshly milled black pepper
  3 oz (90 g/6 tablespoons) butter
  3 tablespoons cooking oil
  ½ pint (0·28 litres/1¼ cups) barley wine
  ¼ pint brown sauce (see recipe under Tripe and Onions, Drake's
    Restaurant, London section)
  about 4 teaspoons redcurrant jelly
  1 finely diced carrot
  1 finely diced medium onion

Pass the chicken through flour, egg and oatmeal. Shake off surplus. Heat the butter in a suitable pan, add the oil and the chicken pieces and cook till golden brown and tender. Remove to a dish, keep warm. Pour off excess fat from pan, add the carrot and onion, soften, add barley wine and reduce to a third. Stir in the brown sauce and simmer to the required consistency. Check seasonings and add redcurrant jelly to taste. Strain sauce and serve. You can, if you prefer make the sauce first.

GOLDEN LION HOTEL (B)

Market Place, Leyburn, North Yorkshire
Tel: Leyburn 2161
Open 12 noon to 2 pm; 7 pm to 9.30 pm

Leyburn, in the Yorkshire Dales, can claim to be one of England's oldest villages since it is recorded in the Domesday Book. There's been an inn in the Market Place in the centre of the village for several centuries, once known as 'The People's Inn', officially christened in 1857 the Golden Lion Hotel.

Under Steve and Audrey Stephenson's management, the hotel has been refitted with modern comforts though manages to retain its old-fashioned character. The dining room offers a number of home-made classic English dishes, along the lines of Roast Ribs of Beef, Yorkshire Pudding with Onion Gravy, Syllabub and local cheeses on the daily menus.

For residents, there is private fishing available at Richmond nearby, and pony trekking by courtesy of an agreement with Lady Masham from Swinton Castle. This is lovely walking country and the Dales are sprinkled with fine old buildings and ruins of historical interest for visitors with cars.

RECIPES FROM GOLDEN LION HOTEL

Creamed Sweetbreads

For 4 people
   1 lb (480 g) calves' sweetbreads
   2 teaspoons lemon juice
   ½ pint (0·28 litres/1⅓ cups) milk
   1 small chopped onion
   a few peppercorns
   1 small piece of celery stalk
   1 oz (30 g/2 tablespoons) butter
   1 oz (30 g/¼ cup) flour
   ¼ teaspoon finely grated lemon rind
   a little salt and freshly ground black pepper
   3–4 tablespoons double cream
   4 slices hot buttered toast

Soak the sweetbreads in lukewarm salt water for 1 hour. Drain and put them into a saucepan with cold water to cover and the lemon juice. Bring slowly to the boil and boil for 5 minutes. Drain and immerse in cold water until cold enough to handle, then cut away gristle and tissues. Bring the milk to the boil, reduce the heat and add the sweetbreads, the onions, peppercorns and halved celery stalk. Let it all simmer for 15–20 minutes. Strain the sweetbread liquor and make up to ½ pint (0·28 litres/1⅓ cups) by adding cold milk if needed. Melt the butter in a clean pan and stir in the flour; cook for 2 minutes without browning and gradually blend in the sweetbread liquor and the lemon rind. Cook, stirring, until the sauce comes to the boil and thickens. Add sweetbreads and season to taste. Heat gently for 5 minutes and stir in the fresh cream. Serve immediately on hot buttered toast.

Yorkshire Cheesecake

For 6 people

The pastry:
> *8 oz (240 g/2 cups) plain flour*
> *4 oz (120 g/½ cup) butter*
> *pinch of salt*
> *water to mix*

The filling:
> *½ lb (240 g) curd cheese*
> *1 oz (30 g/2 tablespoons) softened butter*
> *1 large beaten egg*
> *1 tablespoon caster sugar*
> *1 tablespoon golden syrup*
> *1 oz (30 g/just under ¼ cup) currants*
> *1 tablespoon rum*

Make the pastry by rubbing the butter into the sieved flour and salt. Bind to a paste with the water, roll out and line a flan ring. Mix all the ingredients for the filling and spoon into the pastry base. Bake in the centre of the oven at Gas Mark 6 (400°F/200°C) for about 30 minutes or until filling is firm and golden. This is best served still warm.

GOLDEN LION HOTEL (B)

Market Place, Northallerton, Yorkshire
Tel: Northallerton 2404
Open 7 pm to 9.45 pm

Built as a coaching inn in 1709 and well situated in the Market Place of Northallerton, the Golden Lion has always had a reputation for good food and comfort. By the middle of the nineteenth century it was considered one of the best inns on the London to Edinburgh route. Today it is equally popular with locals and visitors to the area.

Yorkshire is a region famous for good simple food based on fresh ingredients. Many local specialities are offered by the Golden Lion. Yorkshire pudding is served Yorkshire fashion, before the meat with onion gravy; there is fish from Whitby, local hare and pigeons, and the delicious local cheese, Wensleydale, is used to stuff chicken breasts. There are puddings laced with Brontë liqueur produced in Leeds and coffee comes with sweetmeats from Harrogate. We like their lamb steak with honey, mint and lemon and hope that you will too.

RECIPE FROM GOLDEN LION HOTEL

Lamb Steak Wapentake

For 5–6 people
    1 boned leg of lamb cut into 5 or 6 steaks
    ¼ pint (1·5 decilitres/⅔ cup) oil
    ⅛ pint (0·75 decilitres/¼ cup) red wine
    1 bay leaf
    a little mint
    black peppercorns
    5 tablespoons mint sauce
    5 oz (150 g/10 tablespoons) butter
    about ¼ pint (1·5 decilitres/⅔ cup) clear honey
    salt and pepper
    juice of large lemon

Marinate the lamb in the oil and wine with the bay leaf, mint and pepper-corns for about 2 days in a cool place. Then remove meat from the marinade, drain and dry well on kitchen paper. Melt the butter in a pan until a nut brown colour, add the steaks and cook for a few minutes on either side until golden brown outside but still pink in the middle. Remove meat to a hot serving dish. Pour excess fat out of pan and add the honey, the lemon juice and the mint sauce, cook till all are amalgamated, season, pour over the meat and serve at once.

RED LION INN

South Stainley, Nr Harrogate, North Yorkshire
Tel: Harrogate 770132
Open 12.30 pm to 2 pm; 7.30 pm to 9.15 pm (Restaurant);
6 pm to 9.30 pm (Buttery)

The Red Lion Inn has been synonymous with good English food for fifty years. Fifty years in the ownership of the same family, the Fawcetts. It is ideally situated for getting fresh fish from the coast and game from the Yorkshire moors, and as the Fawcetts grow their own vegetables, they have the ingredients to produce varied and imaginative menus, accompanied by an extensive wine list of over a hundred bins. Whether you choose from the menu in the Restaurant or eat à la carte in the Buttery which specialises in fresh seafood, you will find the same degree of comfort and impeccable service from smart and pleasant girls. The Red Lion is in a beautiful part of the Yorkshire Dales, midway between Harrogate and Ripon and only a few miles from one of England's most romantic monuments, Fountains Abbey in Studley Park.

RECIPES FROM RED LION INN

Home-made Veal and Ham Pie

For 6 people

The filling:
  1½ lb (720 g) pie veal
  8 oz (240 g) cooked ham

1 bay leaf
1 small onion
pinch of thyme
salt and freshly ground black pepper
a little parsley
aspic jelly

The short-crust pastry:
8 oz (240 g/2 cups) plain flour
4 oz (120 g/½ cup) butter, or 2 oz (60 g/4 tablespoons) each of
lard and margarine
pinch salt
water to mix

Make the pastry by working the fat into the sifted flour and salt and binding with water to a malleable paste. Leave on the side. Partly boil the cubed veal with the bay leaf and onion in enough water to cover, skimming off any scum – about 1¼ hours. Let veal cool, then cut it and the ham into small cubes. Return both meats to the stock, add the thyme, parsley, salt and pepper and cook for another 15 minutes. Make up aspic jelly using the stock. Put meat in one oven-proof dish or individual dishes, add the jelly and leave to cool. Roll out pastry, cut out a lid or lids, cover the pie dishes, brush with egg and cook in the oven at Gas Mark 4 (350°F/180°C) for about 40 minutes or until nicely browned. Leave to cool.

Fresh Peach Sorbet

For 6 people
9 peaches
¾ pint (0·42 litres/2 cups) water
6 oz (180 g/¾ cup) sugar
½ lemon

Make a syrup with the water, sugar and lemon juice. Leave to stand for 24 hours. Drop the peaches into boiling water, skin and stone them. Purée the peach flesh with the syrup in the liquidiser, boil and then leave to cool. Freeze in the freezing compartment of the refrigerator.

GOLDEN FLEECE HOTEL (B)

Market Place, Thirsk, North Yorkshire
Tel: Thirsk 23108
Open 12 noon to 2.15 pm; 7 pm to 9.15 pm

The Golden Fleece is a welcoming, seventeenth-century coaching inn overlooking the cobbled market place of Thirsk. Twice a week there's the bustle of market people setting up their stalls, and shoppers looking for the freshest – or the cheapest – goods on offer. In company with several of the old buildings round the square, the hotel wears a coat of ivy.

Inside, oak panelling, open fires and low ceilings await visitors. Some of the twenty bedrooms overlook the square; the reception rooms, including a large lounge on the first floor, are comfortably furnished, with antiques and interesting old prints.

The daily menu specialises in local Yorkshire fare – Split pea with York ham soup; Swaledale Lamb steak; Love in a Mist pudding made with local Brontë liqueur, as well as the dishes for which we give recipes here.

RECIPES FROM GOLDEN FLEECE HOTEL

Haddock in a Blanket

For 4 people

The pancakes:
  5 oz (150 g/1¼ cups) plain flour
  1 egg
  ⅔ pint (0·38 litres/just over ¾ cup) milk
  1 oz (30 g/2 tablespoons) butter
  salt
  a little grated cheese for topping
  1 oz (30 g/2 tablespoons) butter for topping
  chopped parsley and lemon wedges to garnish

The filling:
  ½ lb (240 g) smoked haddock fillet
  2 hard-boiled eggs

¼–½ pint (1·5 decilitres–0·28 litres/⅔–1¼ cups) milk
salt and freshly ground black pepper
a little chopped parsley
¼ pint (1·5 decilitres/⅔ cup) double cream
a little lemon juice

First make the pancake batter by beating the egg and half the milk and the melted butter into the flour and salt. Beat well, then add rest of milk slowly, or blend all ingredients in the blender. Leave batter to rest for about 1 hour. Poach the smoked fish in the seasoned milk. When cooked, flake the fish, skin it and remove any bones. Blend the fish with the chopped hard-boiled eggs, a little chopped parsley, the double cream and about ⅓ pint (0·19 litres/just under 1 cup) of the fish stock. Season with ᷂ lt, pepper and a little lemon juice. Put a little of the mixture on each pancake, roll up, put in a buttered fire-proof dish, sprinkle a little cheese on top and dot with butter. Glaze under a hot grill and serve with chopped parsley and lemon wedges.

Drunken Bullock

For 1 person
    A 7 oz (210 g) sirloin steak
    ½ small sliced onion
    1½ oz (45 g/3 tablespoons) butter
    1 oz (30 g) mushrooms
    1 dessertspoon whisky
    4 tablespoons barley wine
    3 tablespoons gravy or brown sauce
    salt and freshly ground black pepper
    a little parsley for garnishing

Season the steak and brush with a little oil, leave on the side while you prepare the sauce. Melt the butter in a pan, add the sliced onion and cook until golden brown. Add the sliced mushrooms and the whisky, then stir in the barley wine and let sauce reduce. Add the gravy or brown sauce and simmer until it thickens. Check seasonings. Keep warm and grill the steak as you like it. Then place steak in pan with sauce, bring to boil and serve at once, topped with a little parsley.

LINTON SPRING RESTAURANT (C)

Sicklinghall Road, Wetherby, Yorkshire
Tel: Wetherby 65353
Open 12.30 pm to 2.30 pm; 7.30 pm to 10.30 pm
Closed all day Monday, Sunday evening and Saturday lunch – except for wedding receptions.

This charming house set in extensive grounds has two restaurants: one specialises in fondues, the other has an extensive and imaginative menu which changes with the seasons but has a permanent house speciality of roast ribs of beef, freshly cooked and carved for you at the table.

The main restaurant is relaxing and comfortable with panelled walls, sparkling white cloths and fine views of the grounds. Linton Spring also run an intimate 'disco' licensed until 2 am, which is very popular in the area.

RECIPES FROM LINTON SPRING

Cream of Carrot and Orange Soup

For 4–6 people
1 lb (480 g) carrots
2 oz (60 g/4 tablespoons) butter
1 large onion
the juice and zest of 1 large orange
1 oz (30 g/2 tablespoons) brown sugar
1½ pints (0·85 litres/4 cups) chicken or vegetable stock
¼ pint (1·5 decilitres/⅔ cup) cream
salt and black pepper

Sweat the onions in the butter until transparent, chop the carrots and cook in the butter for about 10 minutes, add the juice and zest from the orange and the stock. Boil until the carrots are well cooked. Liquidise the contents of the pan and pass through a strainer or fine sieve. Add the cream, the brown sugar and season with salt and pepper. If the soup is too thick, thin it with a little milk. Serve with croutons of fried bread.

Strawberry or Fruit Cocotte

For 4 people
8 oz (240 g) fresh strawberries (or other fruit)
4 measures of any orange based liqueur
¼ pint (1·5 decilitres/⅔ cup) of double cream
a little caster sugar
brown sugar to cover

Cut the strawberries into quarters, sprinkle with the caster sugar and marinate them in the liqueur for about an hour. Place the fruit with the liqueur into ramekins, whip the cream until stiff, fill the dishes to the top with the cream and level it off with a palette knife. Completely cover the cream with brown sugar. Chill the ramekins, then either place the ramekins under a very hot grill for a few minutes until the sugar caramelises or use the method the restaurant uses – heat a sharpening steel over an open flame for an hour. When ready to serve the pudding roll the red-hot steel over the sugar topping. This caramelises the sugar, forming a hard crust. Serve immediately.

HEART OF ENGLAND

Gloucestershire, Hereford and Worcester, Shropshire, Staffordshire, Warwickshire, West Midlands

THE ELMS HOTEL AND RESTAURANT (B)

Abberley, Worcestershire
Tel: Great Witley 666
Open 12.30 pm to 2.30 pm; 7.30 pm to 9 pm (last orders)

In an area rich in beautiful houses, the Elms more than holds its own. Designed by Gilbert White, a pupil of Sir Christopher Wren, and built in 1710 it is surrounded by twelve acres of its own parkland. Additional wings were added in the twentieth century but they blend in discreetly with the Queen Anne façade of the old house. This happy combination of old and new is found throughout the hotel. The twenty charming bedrooms, furnished with antiques, all have private bathrooms, colour TV and telephones, and fabulous views over the grounds. Of the public rooms the bar is housed in what used to be the library of the house; in fact the fine old mahogany bookcases are still there, as well as the original mantelpiece. An open log fire is kept burning all the year in the spacious lounge hall and the Regency style dining room, candle-lit in the evenings, is a fitting setting for the fine food and wine served in the hotel.

The grounds offer formal gardens for sitting in the sun, and tennis courts, croquet and putting lawns for the more active. So varied and interesting is the food that we have taken four recipes – all are simple to make, and offer unusual combinations of flavours, like the Watercress and Almond Soup and the Duckling with Mint and Lemon, lovely fresh flavours to offset the richness of the duck.

RECIPES FROM THE ELMS HOTEL

Stilton and Port Mousse

A delicious starter for a dinner party – it's quick to make and can be done in advance.

For 5–6 people
    ½ lb (240 g) Stilton cheese
    1½ oz (45 g/3 tablespoons) butter
    a sherry glass of port wine
    salt and freshly ground pepper to taste

Beat the Stilton and butter together till creamy; *slowly* pour in the port wine (take care not to curdle). Season to taste and put in individual ramekins. Keep covered in the refrigerator until needed. Serve with hot toast.

Watercress and Almond Soup

This is a lovely soup with an unusual flavour and texture.
For 4–5 people
    1 bunch of watercress
    1 small onion (chopped)
    1 oz (30 g/2 tablespoons) butter
    1 tablespoon flour
    ¾ pint (0·42 litres/2 cups) good white stock
    ½ pint (0·28 litres/1⅓ cups) milk
    4 oz (120 g/¾ cup) ground almonds

Soak the almonds in the milk. Wash the watercress and shred it finely. Melt the butter, add the watercress and onion. Cover and stew gently for 10 minutes. Draw aside and blend in the flour, pour on the stock and bring to the boil. Add the almonds and milk and boil for about 10 minutes. Season, blend or sieve, taste for seasoning. Before serving add a couple of tablespoons of cream. Serve with croutons of fried bread.

Roast Duckling with Mint and Lemon

This is a delicious way to serve duck, the freshness of the mint and lemon providing a lovely contrast to the richness of the duck.

For 4 people
    A 4–5 lb (1·92–2·40 kg) duckling
    1 tablespoon chopped mint
    1 teaspoon sugar
    2 oz (60 g/4 tablespoons) butter
    grated rind and juice of 1 lemon
    salt and freshly ground pepper
    ¼ pint (1·5 decilitres/⅔ cup) stock

To garnish:
  1½ lemons, sliced
  1 bunch watercress

Mix half the chopped mint with the sugar, 1 oz butter, the grated lemon rind and the seasoning. Place this mixture inside the duck; rub the remaining butter over the breast of the duck. Place in roasting tin, pour half the stock round it and roast in a moderately hot oven, Gas Mark 6 (400°F/200°C) basting frequently for about 1–1½ hours, or until duck is cooked (to test, prod the fattest part of the leg with a skewer; juices run clear when bird is done). Take duck out and keep warm. Tip off excess fat from roasting tin, pour in the rest of the stock, plus the lemon juice and boil up, season and strain. Add the rest of the chopped mint and pour sauce over the duck; garnish with lemon slices and watercress.

Fluffy Caramel

For 6 people
  5 egg whites
  8 oz (240 g/1¾ cups) caster sugar
  few drops vanilla essence

The caramel:
  ¼ lb (120 g/½ cup) granulated sugar
  5 tablespoons water

For garnishing:
  whipped cream
  a few flaked and browned almonds

Cook the sugar and water for the caramel until golden brown, pour into a 3-pint soufflé dish. Beat the egg whites as for meringues, add the sugar and vanilla essence. Put the meringue mixture into soufflé dish with caramel and cook in a pan of water in oven for about 1 hour at Gas Mark 5 (375°F/190°C). Remove from the oven and turn out onto serving dish. Pour any remaining caramel over, cool and garnish with whipped cream and the flaked almonds which you have browned in the oven for 5 or 10 minutes. If the caramel has hardened too much to pour, warm it a little. If the meringue breaks when you turn it out, don't worry: mask it with whipped cream – it will taste just as good.

THE SWAN HOTEL (B)

Bibury, Cirencester, Gloucestershire
Tel: Bibury 204
Open 12.15 pm to 1.45 pm; 7.15 pm to 8.45 pm

An old inn of mellow stone smothered in creepers, against a backdrop of fine old trees and facing a clear and gentle river – the position of the Swan Hotel could hardly be improved. Bibury is a charming village of early eighteenth-century stone houses, set in the heart of the Cotswolds. It is ideal walking country and trout fishing is available in the hotel's own stretch of the River Coln (fed by a spring in the hotel garden).

The main part of the hotel was built in the eighteenth century. It soon became a well-known coaching inn, especially after the building of the bridge – until then the local cattle had had to wade across the freezing water. Its heyday was in the days of Charles II, who patronised the famous Bibury Races which moved there from Burford at the end of the seventeenth century. In the days of mail coaches, the Swan also handled the local post and you can still read 'Post Office' in faint Victorian lettering on the left of the main entrance.

Today the hotel has a well-deserved reputation for quiet comfort, friendly efficient service and excellent food with emphasis on good English fare. From the varied and interesting menu we have chosen two house specialities – the Attereau of Tongue and Mushrooms in Madeira Sauce which was a favourite of Mary Queen of Scots, and Bibury Chowder, a delicious fish soup with vegetables.

Bibury Chowder

For 4–6 people
  1 red pepper, de-seeded and diced
  1 green pepper, de-seeded and diced
  1 onion, chopped
  1 large potato, diced
  ¼ stick of celery, chopped
  6 button mushrooms, sliced
  pinch of tarragon
  pinch of dill weed
  4 oz (120 g/½ cup) butter
  4 oz (120 g/1 cup) flour
  1 pint (0·57 litres/2⅔ cups) water
  1 pint (0·57 litres/2⅔ cups) milk
  4 oz (120 g) hake
  4 oz (120 g) mussels
  4 oz (120 g) cockles
  4 oz (120 g) Queen scallops
  2 oz (60 g) prawns

Sauté the vegetables in the butter until soft, but not coloured. Stir in the flour, being careful not to let it brown, then add the water and the milk gradually with the herbs and cook gently for 15 minutes, stirring from time to time. Lastly add the fish and simmer for a further 10 minutes, then serve with a tablespoon of cream per person and garnish with a prawn in the shell and chopped parsley.

Attereau

This delicious dish was a great favourite of Mary Queen of Scots. It makes an unusual starter for a dinner party, or in larger quantities a good main course with a green salad.

For 4–5 people
  15 button mushrooms
  10 cubes of ox tongue (the same size as the mushrooms)
  *½ pint (0·28 litres/1¼ cups) white sauce flavoured with a little
    sherry and bound with an egg*
  white breadcrumbs

a little flour
fat for deep frying

Thread the mushrooms and pieces of tongue alternately on skewers, roll in flour, then coat with the white sauce mixture and finally the breadcrumbs, fry in deep fat until golden brown. Serve with deep fried parsley and a Madeira sauce (see Poussin recipe from Crosby Lodge Hotel in Cumbria section).

THE LYGON ARMS (B, C)

Broadway, Worcestershire
Tel: Broadway 2255
Open 12.30 pm to 2 pm; 7.30 pm to 9.15 pm

The picture-book village of Broadway is probably the most famous in England. At its heart stands the Lygon Arms, an inn since the days of Henry VIII and now so popular with overseas visitors that in 1971 it became the first country hotel to win one of the coveted Queen's Awards to industry.

For several hundred years it was called the White Hart – the badge of King Richard II who died in 1400 – and one of the old bedrooms has a fireplace of fourteenth-century workmanship. The Cromwell Room is still much as it was on that September night in 1651 when Oliver Cromwell is said to have slept in it before the battle of Worcester.

The hotel's links with the past are reflected in the fine antique furniture in the rooms. The Great Chamber has a four-poster bed dating back to 1620 and two tables in the Great Hall are illustrated in the Dictionary of English Furniture. Guests have the peace offered by three acres of garden and a varied menu which changes every week and has a rich choice of both English and international dishes.

RECIPES FROM THE LYGON ARMS

Stilton and Guinness Mousse

For 8–10 people
   8 oz (240 g) ripe Stilton cheese
   1¼ lb (600 g) cream cheese
   2½ tablespoons sour cream
   ¼ pint (1·5 decilitres/⅔ cup) Guinness
   ¼ oz (8 g /¾ tablespoon) gelatine
   pinch cayenne

Dissolve the gelatine in a very small amount of warm water. Slowly beat together the Stilton, sour cream and about ¼ lb (120 g) of the cream cheese. Boil the Guinness until reduced by about half, add the dissolved gelatine slowly. Slowly beat in the cheese mixture with the rest of the cream cheese. Add cayenne to taste. Place in individual moulds and leave to set in a cool place all day or overnight. Turn out to serve or leave in ramekins.

Burnt Cream

For 4–6 people
   4 egg yolks
   1 level tablespoon caster sugar
   1 pint (0·57 litres/2⅖ cups) double cream
   vanilla pod or a little vanilla essence
   caster sugar to cover

Mix the yolks well with the sugar. Put the cream and vanilla pod together in a double saucepan. Cover and bring to scalding point, then remove pod and pour cream onto yolks, blending well. If you are not using a vanilla pod add the essence at this stage. Return the mixture to pan and put it on a low heat, stirring continuously until it thickens – on no account let it boil, scalding point is enough. Strain into a shallow fireproof flan dish that will fit under the grill and leave to stand for several hours or better still overnight .Two to three hours before serving heat the grill, dust the surface of the cream evenly with caster sugar so that it is uniformly covered, but avoid getting too thick a layer. Push the dish under the grill, allow sugar to melt and take colour; watch all the time at this stage. Remove from heat and stand in a cool place for 2–3 hours before serving.

Old English Cider Cake

For 8–10 people
  4 eggs
  8 oz (240 g/1 cup) butter
  8 oz (240 g/1 cup) granulated sugar
  10 oz (300 g/2½ cups) plain flour
  baking powder
  cinnamon
  ½ pint (0·28 litres/1¼ cups) 'scrumpy', or dry cider
  1 dessert apple, 3 cooking apples

Blend the cinnamon and baking powder with the sifted flour. Cream the butter and sugar, beat in the whole eggs, one at a time. Add a little of the flour mixture and a little cider to the egg and butter mixture alternately until everything is blended – use only half the cider. Pour the sponge mixture into a greased and floured sponge flan tin and bake in a moderate oven, Gas Mark 4 (350°F/180°C) for about 30 minutes or until golden brown and firm to the touch. Turn out and allow to cool. Meanwhile purée the apples with the rest of the cider and sugar to taste; when cold place in the middle of the flan. Decorate with slices of dessert apple and a cider glaze, made by thickening cider with a little arrowroot.

THE COTTAGE OF CONTENT (B)

Carey, Herefordshire
Tel: Carey 242

Open 7.45 pm to 11.30 pm
Bar meals every lunch time and evening up to 9.30 pm
Closed Tuesday (except to residents)

A small fifteenth-century inn in the midst of the beautiful Wye Valley, the Cottage of Content lives up to its name. There are only two double bedrooms and the lucky guests will find rural peace and modern amenities like central heating and electric blankets.

The inn was originally built in 1485 as three labourers' cottages, when it was a condition that one of the tenants should maintain an ale and cider parlour in one room – the Cottage has been a licensed house ever since. Today there are two bars, with beautiful oak beams and traditional draught beer – a happy meeting place for locals as well as holidaymakers.

The restaurant boasts unique post beams and seats twenty-four. The owners, Mr and Mrs Roberts, have a sensible policy of accepting only one booking per table per evening from 7.45 pm to 8.30 pm – so no-one feels hurried and there is no panic about being ten minutes late. The same commonsense attitude governs the choice of food. The menu changes every day, according to what is fresh and available, what there is in the larder and the mood of the cook – Mrs Roberts! They believe that it is better to do a few things really well instead of sporting a long and pretentious menu. From the Cottage of Content we give you the recipe for Apricot and Walnut Soufflé.

RECIPE FROM THE COTTAGE OF CONTENT

Apricot and Walnut Soufflé

For 4 people
*½ lb (240 g) dried apricots, covered in cold water and left to
    soak overnight*
4 eggs
4 oz (120 g/just under 1 cup) caster sugar
¼ pint (1·5 decilitres/⅔ cup) double cream
½ oz (15 g/1½ tablespoons) gelatine
2 tablespoons cold water
1 tablespoon lemon juice
2 oz (60 g/just under ½ cup) chopped walnuts

To decorate:

4 walnut halves and ¼ pint (0·14 litres/⅗ cup) whipped cream

Stew the soaked apricots gently until soft, drain excess liquid and liquid-ise apricots or rub them through a sieve. Stir the lemon juice into the fruit purée and fold in the chopped walnuts. Leave to cool. Dissolve the gelatine by adding it to cold water and standing the bowl over hot water until gelatine is dissolved. Separate the eggs and place the yolks and caster sugar in a bowl over hot water and whisk until thick and creamy. Remove from heat and continue whisking until mixture is cool. Fold in the apricot purée and then the dissolved gelatine. Put into the fridge until the mixture is beginning to thicken. Meanwhile, whisk cream until it is the same consistency as the apricot mixture, beat egg whites until they stand in peaks; fold the cream into apricot mixture and lastly add the egg whites. Pour into individual serving glasses and allow to set in fridge. Decorate with piped cream and walnut halves, to serve.

MALVERN VIEW HOTEL AND RESTAURANT (C)

Cleeve Hill, Cheltenham, Gloucestershire
Tel: Bishops Cleeve 2017
Open 7.30 pm to 9.30 pm
Residents only on Sunday

This handsome stone-built house high on Cleeve Hill calls itself a 'restaurant with rooms'. It has indeed a well-deserved reputation for fine food impeccably served in charming surroundings. It also offers very pleasantly furnished rooms (only seven but all with private bath-rooms) and beautiful views over the Severn Vale to the Welsh mountains beyond. Very close to the elegant city of Cheltenham, it is surrounded by places of interest. To the west lie Gloucester, Tewkesbury and its fine Abbey, and the lovely city of Worcester. Travel a short way north and you come to the village of Broadway and then on to Stratford-on-Avon. A south-easterly direction takes you to Cirencester and Oxford.

The extensive dinner menu offers a choice of truly international cuisine. In keeping with our 'Taste of England' scheme we have chosen for you Pheasant in Red Wine and Mushrooms.

RECIPE FROM MALVERN VIEW HOTEL

Pheasant in Red Wine and Mushrooms

For 4 people
2 young pheasants
4 oz (120 g) belly of pork
4 oz (120 g/¼ cup) butter
2 oz (60 g/¼ cup) flour
12 button onions
6 oz (180 g) button mushrooms
a little chopped parsley
4 tablespoons of brandy
1 pint (0·57 litres/2⅔ cups) red wine
½ pint (0·28 litres/1¼ cups) game stock
salt and freshly ground black pepper
2 bay leaves
2 cloves crushed garlic
1 teaspoon fresh thyme
fried croutons for garnish

Cut the pheasants into two. Melt half the butter in a saucepan and lightly fry the pheasants on each side. Remove and drain. Peel the onions and dice the pork; fry both, then return the pheasant to the pan and flame the birds, pork and onions with brandy. Add the red wine, stock, mushrooms, ground pepper, garlic, salt, thyme and bay leaves. Bring slowly to the boil and put in a covered casserole in the oven at Gas Mark 3 (325°F/160°C) for about an hour, until pheasants are tender. Mix the remaining butter with the flour and mix to a smooth paste. Remove birds and onions to a serving dish and keep hot. Bring the cooking liquid to the boil and add the butter and flour mixture in small pieces, stirring well. Allow to cook for about 4 minutes, then pour over pheasants and decorate with chopped parsley and small croutons.

TARA HOTEL (B)

Upton Hill, Upton St Leonards, Gloucester
Tel: Gloucester 67412
Open 12.15 pm to 2.00 pm; 7.15 pm to 9.45 pm

If you visit the Tara Hotel, in the Gloucestershire Cotswolds, the chances are that you will get personal service from at least one member of the Crown family somewhere along the line, for Richard and Jean Crown are very active resident owners, and they have two sons and a daughter in the business. Paul, the eldest, is restaurant manager; Raymond, who trained at Oatlands Park, is chef, along with Lynn, who was top student of her course at Westminster and – as a result – spent some time cooking for the Royal Family at Windsor Castle.

The Tara Hotel is beautifully positioned in five acres of ground looking out on the Malvern Hills and the Severn Valley. The original old country house, built of local stone, was recently cleverly extended to add more bedrooms, each with a private bathroom, and there is a heated swimming pool for residents.

Gloucester itself is only three miles away and worth at least one day's sight-seeing, when you mustn't miss the famous cathedral (founded by Henry VIII from his ill-gotten gains from churches he had disendowed). You are also within easy reach of the Forest of Dean and the Wye Valley, by car.

Food at the Tara is prepared from fresh ingredients of high quality, and the cooking is enterprising and interesting – like the dishes we give recipes for below.

RECIPES FROM TARA HOTEL

Chicken Breasts with Sage

For 4 people
4 breasts of chicken
4 slices back bacon chopped into cubes
2 teaspoons fresh sage, finely chopped
1 cup single cream
¼ pint (1·5 decilitres/⅔ cup) white sauce
2 tablespoons cooking oil
salt and freshly ground black pepper
a little flour
chopped parsley

Dip breasts of chicken in seasoned flour and sauté in the oil with the chopped bacon until almost cooked. Drain off surplus oil and add rest of ingredients to pan. Simmer together until chicken is completely cooked and sauce has thickened. Serve garnished with chopped parsley.

Bibury Trout with Mussels

For 4 people
4 fresh trout, gutted and cleaned
2 lb (960 g) fresh mussels (out of season use 8 oz – 240 g – frozen mussels)
¼ pint (1·5 decilitres/⅔ cup) double cream
1 small glass medium sweet white wine
1 small onion finely chopped
1 clove garlic crushed
salt and freshly ground black pepper
watercress and lemon for garnish
2 tablespoons cooking oil
a little flour

Scrape the mussel shells clean and place in a saucepan with half the chopped onion and enough water to cover the bottom of the pan. Cook over fast heat, shaking the pan until all the shells are open. Drain. Remove mussels from shells and remove beards. Flour trout and coat with oil, lay on a flat tray for grilling and season. While trout are cooking under hot grill, sauté garlic and onion in a little oil until cooked but not brown. Add wine, mussels, cream; reduce heat and cook until sauce begins to thicken. Place trout on hot serving dish, pour over sauce; garnish with small bunch of watercress and twists of lemon.

THE ANGEL INN (B)

Kingsland, Leominster, Herefordshire
Tel: Kingsland 355
Open 12.30 pm to 2 pm; 7.30 pm to 9 pm (9.30 on Friday and Saturday)
Closed Saturday lunchtime

If you are the first person to book for Sunday lunch at The Angel you may well be asked to decide what the day's roast shall be! Whatever it is it will be good, for Basil and Elizabeth Frost, who own and run the charming sixteenth-century pub, employ a Cordon Bleu cook and know a great deal about food.

All the vegetables are fresh and the menu offers unusual dishes as well as traditional English fare; for instance, the two recipes which we are passing on for Egg and Mushroom Gratinée and Pork Chops in Ginger Ale.

The Frosts looked at forty places before they settled on The Angel. Since they bought it they have converted it carefully in order to preserve the period atmosphere. What was once the lounge bar is now an intimate dining-room; a new kitchen, cold room and beer and wine cellar (the pub offers hand-pumped 'real ale') were added. There is food at the bar at lunch time – a popular choice is the home-made beef and vegetable soup – or grills in the restaurant, a traditional Sunday lunch and the full menu in the evening.

The Frosts also arrange special occasions during the winter; their Scottish Night and Olde English evening proved particularly popular.

RECIPES FROM THE ANGEL INN

Egg and Mushroom Gratinée

For 4–6 people
 8 eggs
 8 oz (240 g) mushrooms
 2 oz (60 g/4 tablespoons) butter
 ½ pint (0·28 litres/1¼ cups) white sauce
 4 tablespoons parmesan cheese
 salt and freshly-ground black pepper

Soft boil the eggs (five minutes in boiling water). Sauté the sliced mushrooms in butter. Make the white sauce with ½ pint warm milk, butter and flour. Add the shelled and chopped eggs and the mushrooms to the sauce. Season. Spoon into ramekin dishes. Sprinkle with cheese and brown under the grill.

Pork Chops in Ginger Ale

For 4 people
4 pork chops
a little brown sugar
2 onions
1 tablespoon tomato purée
2 oz (60 g/4 tablespoons) butter
1 tablespoon flour
½ pint (0·28 litres/1¼ cups) ginger ale

Set oven at Gas Mark 4 (350°F/180°C). Sauté the onions in half the butter till golden brown. Place in a casserole dish; brown the chops on both sides in rest of butter and place on top of onions, sprinkle with brown sugar. Mix tomato purée and flour, add ginger ale, pour over chops, season. Cook in oven for about 1 hour, till chops are tender.

THE FEATHERS

Bull Ring, Ludlow, Shropshire
Tel: Ludlow 2718
Open 8 am to 9.30 am; 12.30 pm to 2.15 pm; 7 pm to 9 pm

Ludlow has been called 'the most beautiful, romantic and historic town in England'. See it on a clear summer day with the sun sparkling on the two rivers that serve it, bathing its Norman castle and lovely church with brilliance, and you will find it difficult to disagree. Graceful bridges span the rivers, and every turn brings you to yet another street full of picturesque black and white buildings.

One of the finest houses in the town is the Feathers, with a magnificent half-timbered façade, pargeted plaster work and distinctive gables. It dates back to at least 1521 and the name can be traced back to the celebrations of 1616 in honour of the Prince of Wales, elder brother of King Henry VIII – the feathers or plumes are the traditional emblem of the Prince of Wales. It has been an inn renowned for its comfort for several hundred years, and today's travellers still find a warm welcome with the addition of modern amenities like private bathrooms, central heating and a varied and excellent cuisine with the emphasis on good English food. The attractive stone and timbered restaurant with its inglenook used to be the kitchens and sculleries. And the original dining room is now the lounge, famous for its beautifully carved mantelpiece and elaborately ornamented plaster ceiling.

RECIPES FROM THE FEATHERS

Shropshire Fidget Pie

For 8–10 people
    1 lb (480 g) green (unsmoked) bacon
    1 lb (480 g) gammon
    1 large sliced onion
    4 cooking apples, sliced
    2 oz (60 g/⅓ cup) brown sugar
    salt and pepper
    about 2 pints (1·14 litres/5¼ cups) stock

The pastry:
    12 oz (360 g/3 cups) plain flour
    pinch of salt
    3 oz (90 g/6 tablespoons) lard and
    3 oz (90 g/6 tablespoons) margarine
    or 6 oz (180 g/¾ cup) butter
    water to mix
    1 beaten egg for brushing pastry
    Alternatively you could top the pie with thinly sliced potatoes instead of the pastry. In this case you will need 2–3 lb (960 g–1.440 kg) potatoes.
Cut the bacon and gammon into bite-size pieces and lay half in a large pie dish. Place a layer of apples and onions over, then the rest of the bacon and gammon and finally the rest of the apple and onion. Season well with salt and pepper, add the sugar and pour on the stock to just

below the uppermost layer. Cover with the pastry, brush with egg and bake for about 45 minutes at Gas Mark 4 (350°F/180°C). If you are using potatoes instead of pastry, cover top of filling with potato slices, dot with butter and cook in the same way.

Ludlow Broth

For 8 people
   1 carrot
   1 small onion
   1 small potato
   1 stick of celery
   1 small leek
   1–2 oz (30–60 g) piece of swede
   2 oz (60 g) peas
   2 oz (60 g) sweetcorn
   2 oz (60 g) barley
   salt and freshly ground pepper
   pinch of thyme
   1 bouquet garni
   4 pints (2·28 litres/10⅔ cups) mutton stock
   1 oz (30 g/2 tablespoons) butter
   1 oz (30 g/¼ cup) flour
   chopped parsley for garnishing

Clean and finely chop the vegetables, except for the corn and peas. Wash the barley and cook it in the stock for about ½ hour (it takes longer to cook than the vegetables). Then cook the vegetables (except corn and peas) in the butter with the flour for a few minutes. Pour on the stock and barley, the peas and corn and the herbs. Cook for 45–60 minutes, until vegetables are tender. Adjust seasoning and serve with chopped parsley.

THE COTTAGE IN THE WOOD (B)

Holywell Road, Malvern Wells, Worcestershire
Tel: Malvern 3487
Open 12.15 pm to 2 pm; 7.15 pm to 9.30 pm

If you stay at the Cottage in the Wood you have not only glorious views over the Vales of Evesham and the Severn to the distant Cotswold hills, but, as the name implies, seven acres of natural woodland to explore.

This Georgian Dower House, high on the Malvern Hills, once belonged to the Duke of Gondolphi. It is small enough to have retained the feeling of an English country house and indeed everything is calculated to make you feel at home. The public rooms, furnished with antiques, have open fires, fresh flowers everywhere, piles of magazines. Each of the twenty bedrooms is decorated in individual style.

The hotel prides itself on its exceptionally good food and carefully-chosen wine list. Within easy reach is the fine old town of Malvern, where George Bernard Shaw lived and that most English of composers – Sir Edward Elgar. A flourishing spa in Victorian days the local Malvern water is still in great demand. Despite its rural seclusion the Cottage in the Wood is within a short distance of two motorways, the M5 and M50, making it an ideal spot from which to visit the surrounding countryside, rich in scenic beauty and places of interest.

RECIPES FROM THE COTTAGE IN THE WOOD

Salmon Baked with Cream and Dill in Pastry

For 8 people
The shortcrust pastry:
8 oz (240 g/2 cups) plain flour
4 oz (120 g/½ cup) butter
pinch of salt
1 egg yolk
a little water

The filling:
1 oz (30 g/¼ cup) flour
1 oz (30 g/2 tablespoons) butter
small glass of white wine
½ pint (0·28 litres/1¼ cups) fish stock (made from fish trimmings)
½ gill (0·75 decilitres/¼ cup) cream
salt and freshly ground pepper
a little cayenne

pinch of dill
2 lb (960 g) salmon, skinned, boned and diced into cubes

Make the pastry by sifting the flour and salt together, rub in the butter and bind with the egg yolk and water if necessary. Leave pastry to rest then roll out to about ⅛ inch and line 8 small moulds. Bake blind in a moderate oven Gas Mark 4 (350°F/180°C) until cooked. Turn out and reserve. Next make a roux from the butter and flour, cook for 2–3 minutes, stirring, moisten with the white wine, add fish stock, stirring until it boils, simmer for ten minutes. Add seasonings, dill and cream. Add salmon; let it cook gently in the sauce. When cooked divide the mixture into the 8 pastry cases, top with hollandaise sauce and brown quickly under a very hot grill:

Hollandaise sauce:
3 egg yolks
½ lb (240 g/1 cup) butter, clarified and warm
salt
2 tablespoons white wine
a little lemon juice

Reduce the white wine by half, add a little cold water, pour this onto beaten egg yolks in the top of a double boiler, or in a bowl standing on a pan of hot water. Whisk over gentle heat till thick, then remove from heat and whisk in the melted butter. Season with lemon juice and salt.

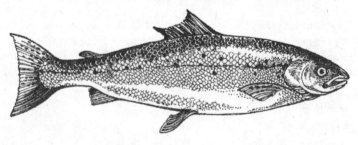

Guinea Fowl Casseroled with Orange, Walnuts and Sherry

For 6–8 people
2 guinea fowl, trussed
the juice of 8 oranges

½ pint (0·28 litres/1¼ cups) grape juice
1 pint (0·57 litres/2⅔ cups) strong tea
½ pint (0·28 litres/1¼ cups) sherry or madeira
40 walnut halves
handful chopped parsley
1 pint (0·57 litres/2⅔ cups) stock made from the giblets
a little oil and butter for cooking
salt and freshly ground pepper
2 oz (60 g/½ cup) flour
2 oz (60 g/4 tablespoons) butter
2 oranges

Season the guinea fowl and brown quickly all over in hot oil and butter in a casserole. Cover with the liquids (orange and grape juice, tea, wine and stock); bring to the boil. Add the walnuts, parsley, salt and pepper and simmer covered for about 45 minutes, or until cooked. Remove birds and walnuts and keep warm. Reduce liquid by one third, then thicken with the flour and butter which have been kneaded together, whisking in a little at a time. Carve the birds, garnish with sliced peeled oranges, walnuts and fine slivers of orange peel which have been blanched to remove bitter taste. Coat with hot sauce and serve.

WALMER LODGE HOTEL (B)

49 Abbey Road, Great Malvern, Worcestershire
Tel: Malvern 4139
Open 7 pm to 11 pm (last orders 9 pm)
Closed Sundays and Mondays to non-residents

A small, quiet hotel, run by a family of skilled hoteliers . . . a chef proprietor who spent five years at the Ritz in London, is a master Craftsman of the Guild of Chefs and a Fellow of the Cookery and Food Association; who was a runner-up in the Chef of the Year competition held in London in 1978 and a prize winner in the 'Heart of England' food competition held in Birmingham . . . Add to this views over the lovely Severn Valley and you see why you have to book well in advance to stay or eat at the Walmer Lodge Hotel.

Maurice Bunton, the chef proprietor, is a creative cook deeply interested in his subject. In the winter, he runs a gourmet club with a new gastronomic menu every month. The menu is repeated sometimes as many as 18–20 times during the month. In Jubilee Year he opened the season with a special menu which included dishes served to Queen Victoria on her Diamond Jubilee and to our present Queen on her Silver Jubilee – they were stuffed quails and fillet of beef with sauce Bearnaise. From Mr Bunton's interesting repertoire of English dishes we have chosen three – a delicious variation on scrambled eggs, brill baked in white wine and a wonderful apricot and almond pudding.

RECIPES FROM WALMER LODGE HOTEL

Old-Fashioned Baked Brill

For 4 people

4 4 oz (120 g) pieces of boned, skinned brill
2 tablespoons chopped onion
1 teaspoon basil
1 good pinch rosemary
1 good pinch thyme
1 good pinch dill weed
1 tablespoon chopped parsley
juice of ½ lemon
1 glass dry white wine (Walmer Lodge use a local wine called
  Three Choirs)
2 oz (60 g/4 tablespoons) butter
salt and freshly milled black pepper
2 tablespoons fine white breadcrumbs

Place the prepared fish into a buttered oven-proof dish, just big enough to take four portions. Season with salt and pepper. Mix all the herbs together with the onion and sprinkle over the fish. Mix the wine and lemon juice and pour over the fish. Cover the dish and let it stand for at least 30 minutes. Then bake in a pre-heated moderate oven, Gas Mark 4 (350°F/180°C) till cooked – 20–25 minutes. Remove the cover, check the seasoning, sprinkle on the breadcrumbs, shake the dish slightly so that the crumbs will soak up some of the stock. Dot with butter and put under the grill to brown.

Regency Apricot and Almond Pudding

For 4 people

The pudding:
12 Boudoir biscuits
½ pint (0·28 litres/1¼ cups) milk
½ teaspoon almond essence
4 beaten eggs
3 oz (90 g/just over ¼ cup) caster sugar
8 whole apricots (fresh or whole canned apricots – canned
*   apricot halves are not suitable as they are too soft to handle*
*   properly)*

The filling:
1 level dessertspoon caster sugar
½ tablespoon butter
½ tablespoon beaten egg (taken from pudding mixture)
12 small macaroons, crushed fine

The glaze:
2 tablespoons apricot jam
¼ measure Apricot Brandy

If using fresh fruit, drop into boiling water for a few minutes, then plunge into cold water to remove skin; remove stones. Make the stuffing by creaming together the sugar and butter. Add the beaten egg, taken from the beaten eggs for the pudding. Mix well, and add the crushed macaroons. Roll mixture into balls about the size of apricot stones and fill the fruit. Place the filled fruit into 4 individual pudding or soufflé dishes, of ¼ pint capacity, which have been buttered and sugared. Then make the pudding. Scald the milk, add the almond essence and pour over the Boudoir biscuits. Allow to soak for 5 minutes, then mash with a fork or put in a blender for a few seconds. Add the sugar and the eggs and beat well. Pour mixture over the apricots, just covering them. Cover the dishes with buttered greaseproof paper and bake au bain marie in a moderate oven for 20–25 minutes, till set. Next make the glaze by melting the jam in a pan, remove from heat and add the apricot brandy; mix well and spoon over the cooked puddings. Allow to cool if you are going to eat them cold, and decorate by piping a rosette of cream in the centre of each dish, put a cocktail cherry in the centre and place split almonds round the cream to resemble a flower.

Martha Eliza's eggs

For each person
2 small eggs
salt and pepper
good pinch of nutmeg or mace
1 oz (30 g) peeled cooked shrimps or prawns
diced fried croutons made from ½ slice of bread
pinch of parsley
1 dessertspoon fresh cream
knob of butter for cooking

Beat eggs, salt, pepper and mace or nutmeg. Scramble in usual way till just setting. Add the warmed fish, complete cooking finishing with cream; add the croutons and serve in a cocotte dish sprinkled with parsley.

MANOR HOUSE HOTEL (B)

High Street, Moreton-in-Marsh, Gloucestershire
Tel: Moreton-in-Marsh 50501
Open 12.30 pm to 2 pm (last orders); 7.15 pm to 9.30 pm (last orders 9.15 pm)
Closed Christmas Day and New Year's Day

This mellow, seventeenth-century manor house, with its lovely walled garden, offers modern comfort, traditional charm and very good food in the middle of the Cotswolds. This is ideal touring country; charming villages amid the rolling hills, old towns with beautiful churches, great houses to visit, music festivals nearby and the Shakespeare season at Stratford-on-Avon.

The original house, in the beautiful local stone, boasts a priest's hiding hole, a secret passage and a bedroom reputed to be haunted! The new wing has been skilfully added on to blend in with the old building; it houses comfortable bedrooms with private bathrooms and colour television and a view of the peaceful gardens.

Both lunch and dinner menus offer a wide choice. We picked three unusual recipes for you to try – the subtle Cream of Carrot and Cauliflower Soup, the Ham and Asparagus Pancakes and a luscious Toffee Ice Cream.

RECIPES FROM MANOR HOUSE HOTEL

Cream of Carrot and Cauliflower Soup

For 8–10 people
  1 lb (480 g) carrots
  2 medium cauliflowers
  white stock to cover (we made it with two chicken stock cubes)
  ½ pint (0·28 litres/1¼ cups) double cream – you can make do with
  half this amount of cream
  1 pint (0·57 litres/2⅔ cups) milk
  salt and pepper

bouquet garni
2 oz (60 g/¼ cup) flour
2 oz (60 g/4 tablespoons) butter

Wash and cut the carrots and cauliflower into small pieces, cook with white stock to cover, with the addition of the bouquet garni, until tender. Make a white roux with the butter and flour, moisten with the stock from the cooked vegetables and the boiled milk, to make a thickish sauce. Either liquidise the vegetables in the blender or pass through a fine sieve and add to the white sauce with the rest of the cooking liquor. Correct consistency of soup with any boiled milk left over from the sauce, adjust seasoning and blend in cream before serving. This is a lovely soup with a delicate flavour, and, like most soups, is better if made the day before.

Ham and Asparagus Pancakes Mornay

For 12 pancakes

The batter:
8 oz (240 g/2 cups) plain or self-raising flour
large pinch of salt
2 egg yolks
1 whole egg
¾ pint (0·42 litres/2 cups) milk
2 tablespoons melted butter

Sift the flour and salt into a bowl, beat to a smooth creamy batter with the beaten eggs, half the milk and the melted butter. Stir in the remaining milk and leave to rest for a couple of hours. Then cook the pancakes until golden brown on both sides and leave to cool.

The filling:
Allow one large slice of ham per person and two or three pieces of cooked fresh asparagus (or frozen, cooked according to instructions)

The cheese sauce:
2 oz (60 g/4 tablespoons) butter
2 oz (60 g/¼ cup) flour
1 pint (0·57 litres/2¾ cups) boiling milk
salt and pepper

1 egg yolk
3 oz (90 g/¾ cup) Cheddar cheese
⅛ pint (0·7 litres/⅓ cup) cream

Melt the butter in a pan, add the flour to make a nice roux, add the hot milk slowly, stirring with a whisk. Add the cheese, salt and pepper. Remove from heat and let it cool slightly, then add the egg yolk beaten with the cream. Cover with foil while you fill the pancakes. Place the pancakes flat, add the ham to each and the asparagus spears and roll up. Put pancakes on a heat-proof dish and stand this over hot water to warm them through. Then cover them with the cheese sauce, sprinkle the top with a little more grated cheese and place under a hot grill until golden brown.

Toffee Ice Cream
For 8–10 people
4 oz (120 g/about 1 cup) caster sugar
3 oz (90 g/6 tablespoons) butter
4 eggs
4 oz (120 g/1¼ cups) icing sugar
¼ pint (0·28 litres/1¼ cups) double cream

First make the caramel by melting the caster sugar over a low heat until it's browned, then melt in the butter. Separate the eggs. Whisk the yolks until well blended, whisk the whites until stiff, beat the sifted icing sugar into the whites a tablespoon at a time, until stiff. Slowly whisk the yolks into the meringue mixture, then the toffee, whisk very hard as you add the toffee, a very little at a time, or it will form lumps as it cools. If it does, scoop it out and melt it again. Then whip cream to soft peaks and fold into mixture. Freeze in a covered container in the freezer compartment of your refrigerator. After about an hour, when half frozen, take out and beat well. Return to freezer until frozen – about two hours.

THE KING'S HEAD HOTEL (B)

High Street, Ross-on-Wye, Herefordshire
Tel: Ross-on-Wye 3174
Open 7 pm to 11.30 pm (last orders 10.30 pm)
Teas, traditional Sunday lunch

There has been an inn on the site of the King's Head for over five hundred years. In a prime position in the lovely old town of Ross-on-Wye, its façade is outstanding in its fine proportions, even in this historic place.

Charles II is said to have patronised it – his is the head on the sign outside – and the two bars are called after him, the King's and the Royalist. Here you can have good snacks at lunchtime; jacket potatoes with a choice of fillings, (chopped ham and sweetcorn, cheese, onion and tomato, savoury mince) a choice of salads and cold platters.

The restaurant offers very well-prepared simple English food, prime roast beef (Herefordshire is beef country) for the traditional Sunday lunch, Mixed Grill, Lancashire Hot Pot and the very good Chicken Pie for which we give the recipe. Ross-on-Wye is set in some of the loveliest countryside in England. The drive along the river to the beautiful ruins of Tintern Abbey is memorable. The mountains of Wales are within a short driving distance, so are the historic cities of Gloucester, Hereford and Monmouth. A lovely spot in which to walk, fish, ride or just look at historic sites.

RECIPE FROM THE KING'S HEAD HOTEL

Chicken Pie

For 4 people

The shortcrust pastry:
8 oz (240 g/2 cups) self-raising flour
pinch of salt
3 oz (90 g/6 tablespoons) margarine
1 oz (30 g/2 tablespoons) lard
cold water to mix

The filling:
3 lb (1·440 kg) roast chicken (this is a good way to use up
*   left-over roast chicken; if you haven't got enough meat add*
*   4–8 oz (120–240 g) quartered mushrooms fried in butter)*
1 oz (30 g/2 tablespoons) butter or margarine
1 oz (30 g/¼ cup) flour
½ pint (0·28 litres/1⅓ cups) milk

84

4 rashers streaky bacon
1 small chopped onion
salt and freshly ground black pepper
2 tablespoons white wine (optional)

Make up the pastry by mixing the fats into the flour and salt and binding with enough cold water to make a pliable paste. Roll out, and line a pie plate, leaving a piece to make a pastry lid. Melt the butter or margarine in a pan, add the chopped onion and let it soften but not colour, add the flour to make a roux and gradually stir in the warmed milk to make a white sauce. Roughly chop the breast and thigh meat from the roast chicken, finely chop the skin from the breast and dice the bacon – add all to the sauce. Season well. If you have just roasted the chicken, skim the fat from the roasting tray and add the remaining jelly to the sauce (you can add 2–3 tablespoons of white wine at this stage too). Pour the chicken in its sauce into the pastry-lined dish and top with a layer of pastry. Brush the top with egg and milk and bake in the oven at Gas Mark 4, (350°F/180°C) for about 40 minutes until nicely browned.

WOODBURN GUEST HOUSE (A)

89 Shipston Road, Stratford-upon-Avon, Warwickshire
Tel: Stratford-upon-Avon 4453
Open to residents only 6 pm to 7 pm (last orders) for dinner prior to theatre performances.

Woodburn is only five minutes walk away from the Shakespeare Memorial Theatre, so dinner is served early to enable theatre-goers to get to the evening performance. The set three-course menu changes every day; the food is English traditional, with regional specialities and dishes evolved by the chef proprietor, David Cunliffe. His creations all have an English flavour and whenever possible he uses only fresh ingredients. A truly imaginative cook, he worked in Grenoble, Monaco and Monte Carlo, and lectured in New Delhi before settling in Stratford-on-Avon.

The day at Woodburn starts with a memorable breakfast: cornflakes, fruit juices or melon in season, grapefruit chilled or grilled with cinnamon and Demerara sugar, or yogurt with fresh fruit. The main course changes daily, and apart from eggs in many forms, bacon, mushrooms and tomatoes, may include Cheese and Ham Pancakes or Derby Toast. As well as toast and marmalade you get one of the following: home-made scones, pancakes, lardy cake, toasted fruit loaf or date shortbread. Small wonder that people keep coming back to Woodburn! From the varied English dinner menu we have chosen the unusual Home Potted Farmhouse Cheddar and Tomatoes served with Savoury Shortbread, the Button Mushrooms in Beer Batter and Crisp Breadcrumbs with Gloucester Sauce, Beef-stuffed Vegetable Marrow and Spring Greens Pie.

RECIPES FROM WOODBURN GUEST HOUSE

Home-potted Farmhouse Cheddar and Tomatoes with Savoury Shortbread

This makes a delicious and inexpensive starter; served in larger quantities with the savoury shortbread it would do very well as a summer lunch dish.

For 6 people (as a starter)
  3 oz (90 g/¾ cup) grated Farmhouse Cheddar cheese
  ½ lb (240 g) ripe juicy tomatoes
  I medium onion, chopped
  2 oz (60 g/⅔ cup) fresh brown breadcrumbs
  I egg
  salt, freshly ground pepper
  a little butter for cooking

Cook the finely chopped onion slowly without colouring in a little butter until soft and remove from the fire. Skin the tomatoes by dipping them into boiling water for about 15 seconds and peeling; remove seeds and roughly chop the flesh. Add to the onion. Add the grated cheese and the breadcrumbs. Mix in the beaten egg and add salt and pepper to taste. Return pan to the stove, bring the mixture to the boil and simmer for 3 to 4 minutes, stirring to prevent sticking. Spoon into small pots, cover and chill. If you are going to keep the pots for any length of time outside a refrigerator then brush tops with melted butter and re-chill.

Savoury Shortbread

For 12–16 biscuits
  6 oz (180 g/1½ cups) plain flour

86

3 oz (90 g/½ cup) ground rice
1 teaspoon salt
4 oz (120 g) Cheddar cheese
6 oz (180 g/¾ cup) softened butter
1 egg yolk
1 tablespoon cream
cayenne pepper
grated nutmeg

Mix together the plain flour, ground rice and salt. Add the grated cheese, and mix in the softened butter. Add the cream and egg yolk and work lightly into the dough until smooth. Press or roll into a round about ½-inch (13 mm) in thickness. Place on a lightly greased oven tray. Dust with nutmeg and a little cayenne pepper, pressing lightly into the surface. Crimp the edges, cut out the centre with a small cutter (eaten as a chef's perk later!) and cut into 12 or 16 'petticoat tails'. Bake in the centre of a pre-heated oven at Gas Mark 2 (300°F/150°C) for 1 hour. Allow to cool for a few minutes and remove to a wire rack until cold. Butter as and if required.

Button Mushrooms in Beer Batter and Crisp Breadcrumbs served with Gloucester Sauce

The batter:
   ½ pint (0·28 litres/1¼ cups) sweet stout (e.g. Mackeson)
   ½ lb (240 g/2 cups) plain flour
   pinch of salt, cinnamon, sugar
   fresh brown breadcrumbs to coat
   oil for deep frying
   allow 2–3 oz (60–90 g) of fresh button mushrooms per person for
      a starter

To make the batter, add the seasoning to the beer and gradually whisk in the flour (eggs are not necessary and tend to toughen the batter when fried). Remove excess stalk from the mushrooms and wash and drain them. Dip them first in the batter and then in the breadcrumbs, coating them well. Deep fry until crisp. Serve sprinkled with chopped parsley, accompanied by the sauce.

Gloucester sauce:

Although this sauce is more traditionally served with cold meat salads, it proves an ideal accompaniment to this dish.

2 hard-boiled egg yolks
I raw egg yolk
¼ pint (1·5 decilitres/⅔ cup) double cream
2 teaspoons lemon juice
2 tablespoons finely chopped chives
I teaspoon Worcester sauce
salt, sugar, cayenne pepper to taste

Pound the hard-boiled egg yolks to a paste with a few drops of water. Stir in the raw egg yolk. Gradually stir in the cream, add the lemon juice, Worcester sauce and seasonings. Finally mix in the finely chopped chives. Leave for 1 hour so the lemon juice has time to thicken the cream to the correct consistency.

Beef-Stuffed Vegetable Marrow

For 4 people

I small, evenly-shaped cylindrical marrow
1½ lb (720 g) stewing beef (weighed after removing excess fat etc.)
4 oz (120 g) streaky bacon (green)
½ lb (240 g) onions
2 cloves garlic
2–3 oz (60–90 g/4–6 tablespoons) butter
2 large tomatoes
I bay leaf
2 dessertspoons flour
Worcester sauce
salt and pepper

The crumble:

2 oz (60 g/½ cup) flour
I oz (30 g/2 tablespoons) butter
I oz (30 g/¼ cup) of English cheese, grated
sprinkling of mixed herbs

To make crumble, simply rub the butter into the flour, add the cheese, herbs, salt and pepper. Remove the ends from the marrow and cut across into sections, about 1-inch (25·4 mm) thick in the centre and about twice as thick towards the end of the marrow where the slices will be of smaller circumference. This should produce about 8–10 slices – 1 or 2 slices per portion, or 3 smaller, thicker ones. Remove the pithy centre part, with the seeds, from the marrow slices (easily done with a grapefruit knife). Melt the butter in a large frying pan, add the finely chopped cloves of garlic and the seasoned marrow rings, simmer covered, as slowly as possible, until nearly cooked but still firm. In the meantime, cut the beef and bacon into tiny cubes. Add the onions, chopped fairly small, a dessertspoon of Worcester sauce, the bay leaf and seasonings. Remove the marrow slices from the pan, turn the heat up, mix the flour into the juices, then add either water or stock to make up about ½ pint (0·28 litres/1⅓ cups). Bring to the boil and pour into this the meats and onions. Simmer until tender. Place the marrow rings onto a greased oven dish, using a perforated spoon; pack each ring fairly tightly with meat mixture, place a slice of peeled tomato on top and sprinkle with the crumble mixture. Heat through when required in a moderate oven, Gas Mark 4 (350°F/180°C) and serve with the gravy and any extra meat around the stuffed marrow.

Spring Greens Pie

This is delicious served either with grilled or roast meats or as a vegetable dish for a first course. The amount of greens required depends on the quality and subsequent amount of wastage, but as a general guide, the following recipe should be adequate for 4–6 servings to accompany a meat course.

2 lb (960 g) spring greens
½ lb (240 g) finely sliced onions
4 oz (120 g/1 cup) grated cheese – use Lancashire, Cheddar, or
  Red Leicester
2 egg yolks
2 oz butter
¼ teaspoon grated nutmeg
salt and freshly ground pepper
fresh breadcrumbs

Cook the finely sliced onions in a little butter, without colouring, until softened. Meanwhile, pare, wash and roughly chop the spring greens and boil in salted water until nearly cooked. Refresh under cold water and drain before chopping finely. Mix together with all other ingredients except the breadcrumbs and place in a buttered, fire-proof dish or individual dishes. Sprinkle with the fresh breadcrumbs and a few small dots of butter and bake in a moderate oven Gas Mark 4 (350°F/180°C) for about 30 minutes. The pie can be prepared well in advance, kept covered in the refrigerator and heated as required. According to the season other varieties of green cabbage, fresh spinach, courgettes, Swiss chard or a combination of these can be used in the same way.

EAST MIDLANDS

Derbyshire, Leicestershire, Lincolnshire,
Northamptonshire, Nottinghamshire

CAVENDISH HOTEL (B)

Baslow, Derbyshire
Tel: Baslow 2311
Open from 7 am for breakfast; 12.30 to 2 pm; 7 pm to 10 pm

What do you look for in a country hotel? A beautiful setting, peace and quiet, good food and service, modern comfort allied to the charm and elegance of another era? The Cavendish offers all that and more. It's in the heart of the Derbyshire Peak National Park, on the Chatsworth Estate (the seat of the Duke of Devonshire) and has been completely re-designed by the Duchess of Devonshire.

There has been a hotel on the site for several centuries. Originally called the Peacock, it belonged to the Duke of Rutland until 150 years ago, when it was taken over by the Duke of Devonshire and run by a series of tenants until 1972. It was then decided to renovate it completely and turn it into a small luxury hotel, re-naming it the Cavendish, the family name of the Devonshires.

The Chatsworth Estate provides fishing for guests on both the River Derwent and the Wye, game for the restaurant and lovely views of the house and rolling parkland from each of the thirteen bedrooms and public rooms. In fact, some of the furnishings and decorations have come from Chatsworth itself. The bedrooms all have *en-suite* bathrooms, colour TV, a clock radio, library and a personal mini bar and hot drinks facilities.

The restaurant offers both international cuisine and traditional English food. Menus are changed periodically to make the most of ingredients in season and are the result of collaboration between the Head Chef, Nick Buckingham, and the proprietor Eric Marsh, who trained at the Dorchester in London and the George V in Paris. There are Taste of England specialities; a number of dishes are available at 24 hours notice and the Chef offers to prepare any dish to order, given adequate notice.

Diners are welcome to visit the kitchen and meet the Chef – all part of making guests feel both welcome and at home.

RECIPES FROM CAVENDISH HOTEL

Honey-roasted Lamb

For 6 people
1 piece best end of lamb
2 oz (60 g/⅓ cup) almonds
6 oz (180 g/¾ cup) clear honey
pinch of thyme
salt and pepper
1 pint (0·57 litres/2¾ cups) gravy

Get the butcher to prepare the lamb, removing the backbone (keep the bones for making stock which you can use as a basis for gravy) and any fat. Cut the best end into 6 pieces, place in a bowl with the honey, thyme, salt and pepper and marinade for 24 hours. Then place in a roasting tin, (with no fat) cover with the honey marinade and cook at Gas Mark 6 (400°F/200°C) for 25 minutes if you like it pink, or 35 minutes if you prefer the meat well done. Five or ten minutes before the meat is ready, put the flaked almonds in a small tin, sprinkle with salt and brown them in the top of the oven. When meat is ready put on serving dish, cover with the almonds and with gravy – we made it simply by pouring well-reduced stock into the juices in the roasting pan, sprinkled with a little flour and salt and pepper.

Farmers' Rabbit Pie

For 4 people
   1 large rabbit
   1 large chopped onion
   8 oz (240 g) sliced mushrooms
   1 pint (0·57 litres/2⅔ cups) brown sauce – to make it see recipe
     for Tripe and Onions, Drake's Restaurant, London section
   ½ pint (0·28 litres/1⅓ cups) red wine
   4 bay leaves
   4 oz (120 g/8 tablespoons) butter
   12 pork meat stuffing balls (we used sausagemeat with fresh
     chopped parsley, the grated rind of ½ lemon, bound with an
     egg)
   salt and pepper

The pastry:
   12 oz (360 g/3 cups) plain flour
   large pinch of salt
   6 oz (180 g/¾ cup) butter or 3 oz (90 g/6 tablespoons) each
     margarine and lard
   2 eggs

Cut up the rabbit into 8 pieces and marinade it in the red wine, the bay leaves, onion, mushrooms and salt and pepper for 2 days. Dry the joints carefully and fry in butter to seal. Add the marinade to the pan and let it bubble until it reduces by half. Add the brown sauce and cook for 1 hour. Check seasonings and leave to cool. Make the pastry by working the fat into the flour and salt and binding with the eggs. Place the rabbit in its sauce in a pie dish, add the pork meat balls, cover with the pastry, egg wash it and bake at Gas Mark 4 (350°F/180°C) for about 40 minutes till nice and brown on top.

THE BLACK HORSE INN (C)

Grimsthorpe, Bourne, Lincolnshire
Tel: Edenham 247
Open 12 noon to 1.45 pm (Monday to Saturday); 7 pm to 9.30 pm (10.30 pm Saturday)
Closed Sunday

The English Shires – Derby, Leicester, Lincoln, Northampton and Nottingham – have contributed a great deal to traditional English food. Bakewell pudding and Melton Mowbray pies come from this part of the country, so do some of our finest cheeses such as Stilton, Leicester and Sage Derby. With this background, it's appropriate to find a lovely country hotel that specialises in English dishes – the Black Horse Inn at Grimsthorpe near Bourne.

Here in a charming rural setting under the shadow of magnificent Grimsthorpe Castle, you can enjoy such local dishes as Fenland omelette, Grimsthorpe Pheasant and Poacher's Game Pot. The Black Horse is leased from the Earl of Ancaster by Mr and Mrs K. S. Fisher, who run the establishment with their eldest son. Since the Fishers took over fifteen years ago, there have been vast changes to the interior of this lovely early Georgian inn. Inside is the feeling of a Georgian country house, with blazing log fires, exposed beams and stone walls. Outside, the walls are covered with bright red pyracantha in the winter and the terrace is a blaze of colour from the tubs of flowers in the summer.

The Fisher family care for their guests in the old-fashioned way. There are fresh flowers in the bedrooms, and Mrs Fisher does the cooking herself. The herbs are all fresh from the walled herb garden and overseas visitors often ask to take back cuttings. If you are staying for a few days there is a lot to see nearby – including Burghley House, the seat of the Marquess of Exeter, Belvoir Castle near Grantham and Peter Scott's Wildfowl Trust at Peakirk.

RECIPES FROM THE BLACK HORSE INN

Stilton Cheese and Herb Pâté

For 4 people
  5 oz (*150 g*) *Stilton cheese*
  5 oz (*150 g*) *Cheddar cheese*

5 tablespoons double cream
1 dessertspoonful mixed herbs
(*thyme, rosemary, basil, sage and parsley*)
1 teaspoon garlic salt

Grate the Stilton and Cheddar finely, add the finely chopped herbs and garlic salt, mix to a soft paste with the double cream. Serve the pâté, garnished with a lettuce leaf and sprinkled with paprika, with thin hot toast.

Elizabethan Pig

For 4 people
8 4-oz (*120 g*) *pork noisettes or 4 lean chops*
1 *large onion*
1 *large cooking apple*
1 *tablespoon Demerara sugar*
3 *tablespoons medium dry cider*
1 *tablespoon chopped parsley*

First prepare the sauce by stewing the apple in a little water till soft, chop and fry the onion in seasoned butter, mix with the apple adding the sugar and cider. Simmer for about 5 minutes. Season the pork and grill on each side, put on a fire-proof dish, coat each piece of pork with two heaped tablespoons of sauce, put under the grill for a couple of minutes before serving. Garnish with a little chopped parsley.

Banana Bernard Shaw

For 4 people
$\frac{1}{2}$ *pint* (*0·28 litres/1$\frac{1}{4}$ cups*) *double cream*
3 *or 4 bananas*
1 *liqueur glass dark rum*
2 *tablespoons 'runny' honey*
2 *oz* (*60 g/just under $\frac{1}{2}$ cup*) *browned split almonds*

Slice the bananas thinly. Whip the cream till thick, slowly add first the honey and then the rum to it; if it gets thin, whip until firm again. Place a layer of bananas in centre of each small serving plate, pipe on a layer of the prepared cream, repeat with two more layers of bananas, finishing with a layer of cream, decorate the top with browned split almonds.

MILL HOUSE RESTAURANT (C)

Covenham, Louth, Lincolnshire
Tel: Fulstow 652
Open 7 pm to 10.30 pm (last orders); 11 pm Saturdays
Closed Sunday

In keeping with the evocative atmosphere of this medieval house, dinner is by candlelight and your pre-dinner drink is served in a gallery bar, overlooking the dining area.

The Mill House is steeped in history; its association with food dates back to the sixteenth century, when it was used as a bakehouse for the adjoining windmill which was destroyed in 1924. The mill ground corn for a Benedictine Priory built on the site by William the Conqueror and destroyed during the Dissolution of the Monasteries ordered by Henry VIII in 1536. All that remained was the bakehouse, which went on baking bread for the neighbourhood until the last war. Some local residents still remember the loaves being delivered by pony and trap.

When the present owners bought it some ten years ago it was in need of restoration. They re-thatched it, extended it and converted it sympathetically into a small restaurant serving good food based on fresh ingredients and making full use of home-grown herbs.

RECIPES FROM MILL HOUSE RESTAURANT

Rook Pie

This is an old Lincolnshire recipe made with young rooks which are shot in May. If you can't get rooks, make it with breasts of wood pigeon and allow at least 1½ hours cooking time instead of ¾ of an hour.

For 4 people
  the breasts off 8 young rooks (or 4 wood pigeons)
  4 slices streaky bacon – beaten out and stretched
  4 oz (120 g) mushrooms
  4 small carrots – sliced
  2 onions chopped
  2 small lamb's kidneys
  2 hard-boiled eggs, sliced
  salt and pepper

chopped parsley for garnishing
about 1 pint (0·57 litres/2⅔ cups) of gravy (if you have any left-
   over from a previous roast, it will do)

The pastry:
   10 oz (300 g/2¼ cups) plain flour
   teaspoon salt
   4–6 tablespoons very cold water
   2 oz (60 g/4 tablespoons) lard
   3 oz (90 g/6 tablespoons) butter
   1 egg

Make the pastry by sifting the flour and salt on a pastry board or work top, make a well in the middle, put the fats in the centre, gradually work the flour in then add the egg and bind to a paste with the water. Roll into a ball and leave for two hours in the refrigerator or a cold place.

Wrap each rook breast in bacon (cut the bacon rashers into strips). Dice the kidneys, cutting out the core and any veins. Sauté the mushrooms, the onions and the bacon-wrapped breasts very lightly in a mixture of oil and butter. Lay half the mushroom and onion mixture in the bottom of individual pie dishes. Add the sliced hard-boiled egg, the rook breasts, chopped kidney and the rest of the mushroom and onion mixture, and the carrots. Season, pour in gravy, sprinkle with chopped parsley.

Bake with a lid on for ¾ of an hour (1½ hours for pigeons) at Gas Mark 2 (300°F/150°C). Take dishes out and cover with a pastry lid, brushed with beaten egg. Increase oven temperature to Gas Mark 7 (425°F/220°C) until pastry is golden – about 15–20 minutes.

HOUSE OF ANTON (B, C)

Castleton Road, Hope, near Sheffield
Tel: Hope Valley 20380
Open 12 noon to 2 pm; 7 pm to 9.30 pm
Closed New Year's Day

The House of Anton is actually the house of Barbara and Anton Singleton. This husband and wife team run a friendly residential hotel and a restaurant which has gained a reputation in the beautiful Peak District National Park for fine English food.

The five-course dinner menu (lunch is three courses from the same menu) changes daily to enable the Singletons to make the most of local produce – they insist on using only fresh ingredients.

We have chosen for you to try the subtle Cream of Orange and Tomato Soup and the Farmer's Fun Casserole – rabbit casseroled in white wine with fresh vegetables and fresh cream. The village of Hope offers holidaymakers facilities for fishing, rough shooting, riding, swimming and golf.

RECIPES FROM HOUSE OF ANTON

Cream of Orange and Tomato Soup

For 6–8 people
> 2 large oranges
> 1 lb (480 g) tomatoes
> 2 medium onions
> 1 can frozen orange juice
> 2 oz (60 g/4 tablespoons) butter
> 4 oz (120 g) tomato purée
> ¼ pint (1·5 decilitres/⅔ cup) double cream
> 2 pints (1·14 litres/5⅓ cups) chicken stock
> salt and freshly ground black pepper
> a little cornflour
> chopped parsley for garnish

Skin the tomatoes by dropping them in boiling water, de-seed them and chop roughly. Finely chop the onions and fry in the butter until translucent. Add the tomatoes and chicken stock and simmer for 10 minutes. Transfer to liquidiser and blend until smooth (or push through a sieve), return to heat and bring to the boil, add the tomato purée and canned orange juice. Take the zest from the two fresh oranges, slice it thinly and add to the soup; squeeze the juice from the oranges into the soup and thicken slightly with cornflour. Add seasonings. Just before serving stir in the cream and serve garnished with orange slices and chopped parsley.

Farmer's Fun Casserole

For 4–6 people
> 3 oz (90 g/6 tablespoons) butter and 1 or 2 tablespoons oil

4 oz (*120 g*) *streaky bacon, diced*
4 oz (*120 g*) *lean shin of beef*
1 *good-sized rabbit, jointed*
3 *tablespoons plain flour*
3 *pints* (*1·71 litres/8 cups*) *veal or chicken stock*
¼ *pint* (*1·5 decilitres/⅔ cup*) *dry white wine*
1 *clove of garlic, finely chopped or crushed*
1 *bouquet garni*
8 oz (*240 g*) *mushrooms, coarsely chopped*
3 *large Spanish onions, chopped*
2 *large carrots chopped*
salt and freshly ground pepper
¼ *pint* (*1·5 decilitres/⅔ cup*) *double cream*

Heat the butter in a heavy pan or casserole. Add the bacon and brown, lift it out with a slotted spoon and reserve. Add the rabbit to the pan and fry until lightly browned, remove from pan and fry the shin of beef in the same way and reserve. Lightly fry onions and carrots and set aside. Stirring constantly, gradually add the flour and cook for about 1 minute. Blend in the stock and wine slowly, add the garlic, the bouquet garni, the rabbit and beef season and simmer for an hour. Add the onions, carrots and mushrooms and bacon to the casserole, cover and cook until tender, (about ½ hour). Just before serving add the cream to the casserole, stirring gently; re-heat and serve immediately.

THE QUEEN HOTEL (B)

323 High Street, Lincoln
Tel: Lincoln 26900
Open 12 noon to 2 pm; 6.30 to 9.15 pm
Closed Sunday

Lincoln Cathedral dominates the city from a high position within the Roman walls. This site dates back to the Norman invasion, but a fire in 1141 and an earthquake in 1185 took their toll on the original Norman structure. Saint Hugh was responsible for the rebuilding in the present Gothic form. Part of the cathedral's treasury is one of only four Magna Cartas in existence.

Lincoln also boasts an eleventh-century castle, and the only Roman gateway still straddling a road in England. The Queen Hotel is a quarter of a mile's walk from the cathedral and the castle, along cobbled streets through the old part of the city. There you will find mainly English food – basically simple – with some regional specialities like the Lincolnshire Pike, for which we give the recipe below.

RECIPE FROM THE QUEEN HOTEL

Pike is a Lincolnshire fish, so it's not surprising to find it on the menu of the Queen Hotel. We give a good way to cook it, but first some general advice on pike from the chef of the hotel.

Try to use small fish, no bigger than 6 lb, to ensure tenderness. Always soak fish in salt water to remove any river odours. Buy fish from a reputable supplier

or

make sure you know which river or lake it came from

or

better still try to catch one yourself! The best fish is caught during the winter.

Poached Pike with Walnut Mayonnaise

For 4 people
   1 3 lb (1·440 kg) pike will yield 4–6 good portions
   2 pints (1·14 litres/5¼ cups) water
   ¼ pint (0·28 litres/1¼ cups) dry white wine
   3 large pinches of mixed herbs
   salt and pepper

The mayonnaise:
   3 egg yolks
   2 tablespoons vinegar
   1 level dessertspoon English mustard
   1 pint (0·57 litres/2⅔ cups) good vegetable oil or olive oil
   4 oz (120 g/¾ cup) diced walnuts
   salt and pepper

Remove the head, tail, fins, skin and stomach contents from fish. Cut into steaks, lengthways, do not remove back bone. Soak in salted water for at least 2 hours. Put 2 pints of water, white wine, herbs and seasonings in a pan, add the fish steaks and bring to the boil. Cover with a lid and simmer for about 15 minutes – the time will vary with the size of the steaks. When cooked, remove steaks from stock and allow to cool.

Make the mayonnaise by mixing the egg yolks with the vinegar, mustard, salt and pepper. Beating continuously add the oil a little at a time until all is absorbed. Mix in the nuts and store in the refrigerator until needed. Serve the pike on a bed of lettuce, garnished with tomato, cucumber and lemon, accompanied by the walnut mayonnaise.

THE FITZGERALD ARMS (B)

Church Street, Naseby, Northamptonshire
Tel: Guilsborough 273
Open 12 noon to 2 pm; 6 pm to 10 pm

This old inn is situated in a historic village in Pytchley Hunt country. It stands on the source of the River Avon, which flows on to Stratford-on-Avon and is within walking distance of the battlefield of one of the most famous encounters of the Civil War – the battle of Naseby in 1645. At the time of the battle there was an old inn on this site, called the Bell.

Mrs Pearson, who now runs the pub, told us she had met a lady whose parents were tenants of the inn in 1918 and who remembered the beer being delivered from Banbury by drays drawn by Shire horses. The draymen would unload and reload their empties, stable the horses overnight at the inn and put up for the night.

Today the Fitzgerald Arms is still a rendezvous for riding parties. It provides very good food – as you will see from the recipes we give you – in a pleasant, warm atmosphere with crackling open fires in winter. There are bar snacks as well as a full à la carte menu and a well-stocked wine cellar.

RECIPES FROM THE FITZGERALD ARMS

Chicken Liver and Mushroom Pâté

For 6–8 people
    4 oz (120 g) streaky bacon
    1 lb (480 g) chicken livers
    4 oz (120 g/8 tablespoons) butter

1 small onion, sliced
1 clove garlic, chopped
2 tablespoons brandy
4 oz (120 g) mushrooms
4 tablespoons stock
1 egg
¼ pint (1·5 decilitres/⅔ cup) double cream
2 tablespoons lemon juice
pinch of thyme
black pepper

Remove the rinds and fry the chopped bacon gently in half the butter with the livers, the garlic and onion until browned. Add the brandy and cook a little longer. Put the liver mixture through the mincer twice, using a fine blade, together with the chopped mushrooms. Mix together with the stock, egg, cream, lemon juice and seasonings. Put in a small loaf or pâté tin, cover with foil and cook in a bain marie for 2 hours, or in a low oven – Gas Mark 2 (300°F/150°C), the tin standing in a tray of water. When cooked, top with the remaining butter which you have melted and leave to cool. Serve cold on a bed of lettuce with hot toast.

Braised Duckling with Olives

For 3–4 people
1 duckling
1 oz (30 g/2 tablespoons) butter
1 medium onion, sliced
1 glass port
1 teaspoon paprika pepper

½ pint (0·28 litres/1¼ cups) jellied stock
bouquet garni
salt and pepper
2 tomatoes
12 large green olives, or green olives stuffed with pimento
1 dessertspoon plain flour

Brown the duck in the butter in a deep casserole; when evenly coloured, tip off the fat and add the onion; cover and cook slowly until the onion is soft. Moisten the bird with the port, allow the liquid to reduce by half, then stir in the paprika and cook for 2–3 minutes. Add the stock and the bouquet garni, check seasonings. Cover the casserole and cook very gently for about 45 minutes or until the duckling is tender; it can be cooked on top of the stove or in the oven at Gas Mark 4 (350°F/180°C). While the duck is cooking, skin the tomatoes by popping them into boiling water, quarter them and remove the seeds, then cut the flesh into neat shreds. If using stuffed olives leave them whole, otherwise cut them in strips off the stones. Blanch them in boiling water for 5 minutes, drain and leave to soak in cold water for 30 minutes, then drain again. When duck is cooked, remove it from the casserole and keep hot; remove bouquet garni, skim fat from liquid; mix the flour with 1 tablespoon of the hot liquid, return this to the casserole and stir until it comes to the boil, let it simmer for 5 minutes, then add the tomato shreds and the olives, reheat, taste seasoning. Cut duckling into portions, and cover with the hot sauce.

Bakewell Tart

For 6–8 people

The pastry:
6 oz (180 g/1¼ cups) plain or self-raising flour
pinch of salt
3 oz (90 g/6 tablespoons) butter or margarine
1¼ teaspoonfuls caster sugar
1 large egg yolk
cold water to mix

The filling:
1 tablespoon strawberry jam
1 tablespoon lemon curd

1 oz (30 g/2 tablespoons) butter
2 oz (60 g/¼ cup) caster sugar
the grated rind and juice of ½ lemon
1 egg
2 oz (60 g/½ cup) ground almonds
2 tablespoons cake crumbs
1½ oz (45 g/⅓ cup) split almonds, chopped

Make the pastry by rubbing the fat into the flour and salt, stirring in the sugar and binding to a paste with the egg and water. Leave it to chill, then roll it out and line a sandwich tin; trim edge and scallop with the thumb. Spread the pastry first with the jam and then with the lemon curd (if you warm them slightly they will be easier to spread). Cream the butter until soft, add the sugar and lemon rind and beat until light. Beat the egg and add it to butter, a little at a time, then stir in the almonds, cake crumbs and lemon juice. Spread the almond mixture over the lemon curd and bake for 35–45 minutes, until set and golden brown, at a temperature of Gas Mark 5 (375°F/190°C). When cool top with the chopped split almonds. Serve cold with cream.

PEACOCK HOTEL

Rowsley, Matlock, Derbyshire
Tel: Darley Dale 3518
Open 12.30 pm to 2 pm (last orders 1.30 pm); 7 pm to 9.30 pm (last orders 9 pm)

With its fine old stone façade covered in climbing roses, a statue of its namesake in the eaves, and magnificent gardens reaching down to the River Derwent at the back, the Peacock has all the evocative charm of an old English country house.

Situated in the pretty village of Rowsley in the Derwent Dale, and built in 1652, it later became the Dower House of nearby Haddon Hall.

Always a fisherman's paradise (Isaac Walton stayed here), it offers guests rainbow trout along a 7-mile stretch of the River Wye and brown trout and grayling along 2 miles of the River Derwent. It also offers charming and comfortable surroundings; bedrooms furnished with antiques and all modern amenities, a friendly bar and a traditional dining-room overlooking the gardens, serving good wines and carefully-cooked food.

The varied menu has many traditional favourites and some new ways of using fresh local produce.

RECIPES FROM PEACOCK HOTEL

Fennel Soup

For 6–8 people
  3 oz (90 g/6 tablespoons) butter
  2 onions
  1 large fennel
  2 medium potatoes
  2 oz (60 g/¼ cup) flour
  2¼–2½ pints (1·28–1·42 litres/6–6⅔ cups) beef or chicken stock
  ¼ pint (1·5 decilitres/⅔ cup) double cream
  salt and freshly ground black pepper

For this lovely creamy soup finely chop the onions, fennel and potatoes; melt the butter in a saucepan and add the vegetables; cover, let them sweat off but not colour. Add the flour, salt and pepper, pour on the stock (we used stock cubes) and let it boil. Leave to simmer till vegetables are cooked. You can then either liquidise the soup or pass it through the mouli, or if you prefer, leave it as it is. Add the double cream (being careful not to let soup boil) and serve.

Braised Lamb's Sweetbreads

For 4 people
  2 lb (960 g) sweetbreads
  4 oz tomatoes (120 g) peeled, de-seeded and roughly chopped
  ½ pint (0·28 litres/1¼ cups) brown sauce (see recipe for it under
    Tripe and Onions, Drake's Restaurant, London section)

$\frac{1}{4}$ lb (120 g) mushrooms
$\frac{1}{2}$ oz (15 g/1$\frac{1}{2}$ tablespoons) juniper berries
1 wine glass white wine

Cook the sweetbreads for 25 minutes in boiling salted water. Crush the juniper berries. Put them in a saucepan with the wine and let it bubble and reduce a little; add the tomatoes and the brown sauce. Quarter the mushrooms and add them, cook for a few minutes, then add the drained sweetbreads, bring to boiling point, check seasoning and serve.

Pot-Roast Shoulder of Veal

For 8 people
6 lb (2·880 kg) shoulder of veal
2 carrots
2 onions
2 sticks celery
pinch of mixed herbs
4 oz (120 g/$\frac{1}{2}$ cup) butter
$\frac{1}{4}$ pint (1·5 decilitres/$\frac{2}{3}$ cup) water
$\frac{1}{4}$ pint (1·5 decilitres/$\frac{2}{3}$ cup) single cream
about $\frac{1}{4}$ pint (1·5 decilitres/$\frac{2}{3}$ cup) gravy
salt and pepper
1 lemon
packet thyme and parsley stuffing

Get the butcher to bone the shoulder of veal, keep the bones to provide stock with which to make the gravy. Make stuffing by mixing the rind and juice of a lemon into thyme and parsley stuffing. Spread stuffing onto veal, roll and tie firmly. Put the meat into a roasting pan containing the water and add the finely diced carrots, onions and celery. Put herbs and small knobs of butter on meat, wrap the joint in tin foil and cook for about 3 hours at Gas Mark 5 (375°F/190°C). Remove the veal from the pan, add the gravy and cream to the juices in the pan, boil up and strain. Serve the veal with the sauce.

THAMES AND CHILTERNS
Bedfordshire, Berkshire, Buckinghamshire, Hertfordshire, Oxfordshire

THE KING'S HEAD AND BELL (B)

East Saint Helen Street, Abingdon, Oxfordshire
Tel: Abingdon 27805
Lunch from 12.30 pm to 3 pm
Dinner from 7.00 pm to 11.00 pm
Closed Sunday night. Also open for breakfast, teas

Abingdon is full of fine old buildings, including the King's Head and Bell where Charles I sometimes held his Councils of War from 1640–1642. All round here was Civil War Country, with the Royalist headquarters set up nearby, at Oxford. Anyone interested in following the bloody trail of battles through the lovely countryside of Bucks, Beds and Oxfordshire should consult a detailed leaflet of places to visit, put out by the Thames & Chilterns Tourist Board.

In calmer days, Handel wrote music at the King's Head and Bell, and the Inn is mentioned in Pepys's Diary. Despite a distinguished past, however, the building was empty for four years in the mid 1970s, until the present owner put it to rights. Now, there are two downstairs bars, with attractive stone walls and floors, and an upstairs restaurant called 'A Taste of England' after the English Tourist Board's scheme. As you would expect, the food is mainly English, and there are a number of good, old-fashioned dishes on the menu.

The dining room is most unusual: it was made by marrying together three small rooms, one up and two down, with an open staircase leading to the area upstairs for drinks before and coffee after your meal. The original oak beams give it great charm. Sunday is an excellent day to take the family, for Chef cooks a hearty set lunch at very reasonable prices. Abingdon is on the Thames, and there are some lovely walks down by the river, if you have time to spare after looking round the town.

RECIPE FROM THE KING'S HEAD AND BELL

Cheese Ramekins

For 4 people
½ pint (0·28 litres/1¼ cups) milk
¼ lb (120 g/1 cup) grated matured Cheddar cheese
1 large egg
2 tablespoons cream
a pinch of nutmeg
salt and pepper

Scald the milk but don't let it boil, beat in the egg, add the cheese, whisking all the time, then the cream and nutmeg, tasting before you add salt and pepper. Place in buttered ramekins, stand them in a tray of hot water and cook them in a moderate oven, Gas Mark 6 (400°F/200°C) for 30–45 minutes, or until the top is firm to the touch. (If you like, sprinkle a little grated cheese on the top and pop under a hot grill for a minute, until brown and bubbling.)

THE CROWN HOTEL (B)

High Street, Amersham, Buckinghamshire
Tel: Amersham 21541
Open 12.30 pm to 2.15 pm (last orders 2 pm); 7pm to 10 pm (last orders 9.30 pm – 9 pm on Sunday)

It's a joy to walk along the main street of Old Amersham and see the lovely cottages and houses on either side, many dating back to early Tudor days. The surrounding area is rich in history, too. There is Disraeli's house at High Wycombe, Milton's cottage at Chalfont St Giles, the red-brick Friends' meeting house at Penn and The Barn at Old Jordans' Farm which is said to contain sister beams to those used in the *Mayflower*.

Amersham is only 45 minutes by road from London, or 45 minutes direct from Heathrow. To anyone visiting the town, we would recommend the Crown in the High Street, opposite the Market Square. There's been an inn for travellers on this site for 400 years – the interior is unmistakably Elizabethan, though the façade is Georgian.

A feature of The Crown are the hot snacks in the very pleasant timbered bar. This benefits from sharing the same kitchen as the hotel restaurant. Indeed, several items are on both menus, like the very good thick home-made soup and the hot Smokies. If the bar is full, the snacks are served in the comfortable lounge. There is a hot dish of the day, soup, individual shepherds' pies, home-made pâté, a very good Crown Rarebit and the traditional Ploughman's lunch as well as fresh sandwiches. The snacks are available only at lunchtime and not on Sundays. The handsome restaurant offers some unusual dishes – Mushroom and Prawn Pot, blended with fresh cream and fennel and Cream of Chicken and Crab soup with toasted almonds – as well as a good choice of fish and shell fish, grills and veal and chicken dishes. Children's portions are half price and prices include service and VAT.

RECIPE FROM THE CROWN

Lentil and Ham Soup

For 6–8 people
1 lb (480 g) split lentils
4 pints (2·28 litres/10⅔ cups) ham stock
2 carrots
1 large onion
salt and pepper
a little butter

This is a nice soup to make if you have gammon and have stock left over; alternatively, make the stock from ham bones. Soak the lentils, then drain well. Soften the sliced onion in the butter, add the lentils and let them absorb some of the butter, then add the stock and the carrots; cook until lentils are soft. Either blend or press through a sieve, or you may prefer to leave the soup really thick. Add a little butter before serving and sprinkle with chopped parsley.

THE BELL INN (C)

Aston Clinton, Buckinghamshire
Tel: Aylesbury 630252
Open 12.30 pm to 1.45 pm; 7.30 pm to 9.45 pm

Few of our readers will need an introduction to the Bell. This handsome, red-brick inn, set in a quiet leafy part of Buckinghamshire, has been famous for its high standards of comfort and cooking since the Harris family took over.

The building dates back to the seventeenth century (when it was probably used as a coaching stop by the Duke of Buckingham) and you can stand on the original stone flags to drink whatever is your preference in a cheerful bar. Rooms in the hotel are luxuriously appointed with fine antiques, and polished silver and cut glass gleam in the dining room.

Only thirty-five miles from London, it's lovely to drive out here on light summer evenings to enjoy a splendid meal. Better still, to stay on for a few days of great comfort in one of the charming bedrooms.

Though the menu features many French dishes, there are traditional English favourites, too: roast beef, the local Aylesbury Duckling, game, when in season, and classic English sweets.

RECIPES FROM THE BELL INN

Bell Inn Smokies

For 4 people
   4 medium tomatoes
   12 oz (360 g) smoked haddock
   ¼–½ pint (1·5 decilitres/⅔ cup – 0·28/1¼ cup) double cream
   freshly ground black pepper

Dip the tomatoes in boiling water, skin and slice them and put them in the bottom of individual ramekin dishes. Flake the smoked haddock and add it to the ramekins, almost filling the dishes. Pour on cream, add freshly ground pepper and either put ramekins in the top of a hot oven, Gas Mark 7 (425°F/220°C) or under the grill until they are bubbling.

Tipsy Cake

This was the forerunner of the modern trifle.

For 6 people
   A 12-oz (360 g) sponge
   1½ measures rum
   1 large wine glass sherry

6 oz (180 g) raspberry jam (seedless for preference)
whipped cream and split almonds to decorate

Place the cut sponge in a mould. Melt the jam gently in a pan and pour it over the sponge, add the rum and sherry and press the sponge firmly into the mould. Refrigerate for 1 hour, turn out and cover with whipped cream, decorate with toasted split almonds.

THE THATCHED HOUSE HOTEL (B)

Sulgrave, Near Banbury, Oxfordshire
Tel: Sulgrave 232
Open 12.30 to 2 pm and 7.30 pm onwards (last orders 9 pm)
Closed Monday evenings

How often, driving round the English countryside on a summer evening, you come upon a lovely old house in an old-fashioned garden and wish that you could stay there!

The Thatched House is such a place – a long low house, the mellow stone topped by one of those thatched roofs that look as though they wear a fringe, with a cottagey garden at the front. Across the road from it is Sulgrave Manor, the handsome ancestral home of George Washington, open to the public and full of interesting possessions.

The hotel and restaurant (which is open to non-residents) are owned and run by a young husband-and-wife team. He does the cooking, she receives guests in the small and pretty bar. It's more like being in a very well-run private house where you are made to feel really welcome and given a delicious meal in charming surroundings. The fine dining room, with flagged floor, exposed beams and a log fire burning in a handsome inglenook, has apple green and gold tablecloths and scarlet candles on the tables.

The food is good and all home-made, from the imaginative hors d'oeuvres to the puddings – a large selection on a trolley: fresh fruit salad in a silver bowl, fresh pineapple, lemon meringue pie, chocolate gâteau and an excellent Apple and Sultana Flan for which we give the recipe.

Main courses (from which we chose the Pork and Apricots for the interesting combination of flavours) come with very good vegetables. We had braised cauliflower, buttered parsnips, duchesse potatoes and a dish of finely sliced potatoes and herbs. Prices are moderate and the service is friendly and efficient. This is a good place from which to tour the Cotswolds and Shakespeare country – the bedrooms have been modernised and are quiet and comfortable; some have private bathrooms.

RECIPES FROM THE THATCHED HOUSE

Pork and Apricots

For 8–10 people
   3 lb (1·440 kg) piece of loin or leg of pork
   a few stoned fresh apricots or dried apricots which have been
     soaked
   origanum, marjoram, parsley, salt and black pepper
   a little butter
   2 sliced onions
   4 sliced carrots
   2 bay leaves
   a little lard or dripping

Ask the butcher to remove the bones from the joint; in the cavity left, place the apricots, sprinkle with the herbs, salt and pepper and cover with thin slices of butter. Roll and tie the joint securely. Place on a bed of sliced carrots and onions, add the bay leaves, rub the joint with salt, and place a little lard or dripping on the top. Roast at Gas Mark 6 (400°F/200°C) for 25 minutes per lb and 25 minutes over. Serve with thin gravy from the juices in the pan. The joint is very good served cold.

Apple and Sultana Flan

We had this delicious pudding cold with cream, but there is no reason why it should not be served hot.

For 8 people

The pastry:
  ½ lb (240 g/2 cups) plain flour
  4 oz (120 g/8 tablespoons) butter
  2 oz (60 g/¼ cup) sugar
  1 egg
  pinch of salt

Sieve the flour with the salt; rub in the butter until you get a sandy texture. Mix the egg and sugar and add to the flour. *Gently* mix until a smooth paste is obtained. Cover with a tea cloth and leave to rest for at least ten minutes. Then fill a flan case with pastry, prick the bottom and fill with the following mixture:

The filling:
  1 lb (480 g) cooking apples
  2 oz (60 g/⅓ cup) brown sugar
  a knob of butter
  a couple of cloves
  1 egg yolk
  2 dessert apples, peeled, sliced and cored
  3 oz (90 g/¾ cup) sultanas soaked in 3 tablespoons rum
  a little caster sugar
  a pinch of cinnamon

Make a purée with the cooking apples, brown sugar, butter, and cloves, then beat in the egg. Let it cool a little and spread it over the base of the pastry. Cover with a layer of sliced apples and the sultanas; sprinkle with caster sugar and cinnamon. Use left-over pastry to make a lattice pattern of thin strips over the top. Cook in a moderate oven, Gas Mark 6 (400°F/200°C) for about 40 minutes, then dust top with icing sugar and glaze under the grill.

THE PLOUGH HOTEL AND RESTAURANTS (A, B,C)

Clanfield, Oxfordshire
Tel: Clanfield 222
Open 8.15 am to 9.15 am; 12.15 pm to 2 pm and 7.15 pm to
10.15 pm; seven days a week throughout the year
Hotel open all day to residents

The Plough is a shining example of how good English food can be and it offers the additional bonus of a beautiful setting. The owners, Harry and Jean Norton, bought this lovely Elizabethan hotel in 1968 and immediately set about renovating the interior of the Cotswold stone building. Keeping the original stone walls and windows they have created three charming dining rooms, particularly attractive in the evening with candles in silver holders on the tables and a colour scheme of forest green, turquoise and white. The entrance lounge bar is welcoming with exposed beams, a large open fire and comfortable sofas and armchairs. Upstairs there are six double bedrooms, one with a four-poster bed.

Mrs Norton is a cook of distinction and, cooking her own recipes, has won prizes in international competitions. She supervises the cooking and the English menu planning together with Colin Cooper English, who gained a '*mention bien*' at the Ecole Hotelière in Lausanne.

'We are fanatical about English food', Harry Norton says, 'and believe that at its best it compares favourably with any other cooking in the world.'

The Plough serves breakfast, lunch and dinner seven days a week and the Nortons also own and run the Plough Tavern, a pub over the road where you can get good bar snacks and toasted sandwiches.

In a sensible effort to simplify bills, every item on the menu carries VAT and service charges built-in and there is no cover charge. The service is pleasant and unobtrusively efficient and the food delicious, prepared from excellent ingredients (their vegetables are grown specially for them) in imaginative but not over-fussy recipes. We give three recipes – Vegetarian Pancake, which you don't have to be a vegetarian to enjoy, a wonderful way with duck served with a wine and cherry sauce and a lovely pudding, Butterscotch Mousse with Grand Marnier.

The Plough is in the heart of beautiful countryside within short driving distance of the city of Oxford and Blenheim Palace and near enough to London to make it possible to drive out for dinner on a summer evening – it is certainly well worth the journey.

RECIPES FROM THE PLOUGH

Vegetarian Herb Pancake

For 8 pancakes

The batter:
  4 oz (120 g/1 cup) plain or self-raising flour
  pinch of salt
  1 egg
  ½ pint (0·28 litres/1⅓ cups) milk
  a little lard or vegetable oil for cooking
  1 teaspoon mixed herbs

Mix flour and salt, make a well in the middle and break in the egg and a little milk, stir mixture well; gradually add half the milk, beat well for five minutes, stir in the rest of the milk and the herbs, leave in a cold place for half an hour. Melt just enough fat to cover the base of a frying pan. When a faint blue smoke rises, pour in a little of the batter, tilting the pan so it spreads to a thin, even layer. Turn or toss when golden brown underneath and brown other side. Remove and keep warm. Make 7 more pancakes in same way.

The filling:

 $\frac{1}{2}$ *lb (240 g) mushrooms*
 1 lb (480 g) courgettes
 2 sweet green peppers (capsicums)
 2 sweet red peppers
 1 large onion
 salt and pepper
 $\frac{1}{2}$ *pint (0·28 litres/1$\frac{1}{4}$ cups) double cream*
 2 oz (60 g/$\frac{1}{2}$ cup) Parmesan cheese
 a little oil for cooking

Dice onion finely and cook in oil until transparent. Cut courgettes into thin strips, slice mushrooms and peppers and add to mixture in pan. Season and cook until tender. Put a little of the mixture and a little cream to one edge of each pancake and roll. Place pancakes in a shallow oven-proof dish. Sprinkle a little more cream over tops of pancakes and a little Parmesan, pop under hot grill for one minute and serve at once.

Butterscotch and Grand Marnier Mousse

For 8–10 people

 1 pint (0·57 litres/2$\frac{2}{3}$ cups) double cream
 3 tablespoons golden syrup
 4 oz (120 g/$\frac{2}{3}$ cup) Demerara sugar
 3 oz (90 g/6 tablespoons) butter
 1 egg yolk
 4 egg whites
 2 tablespoons Grand Marnier liqueur
 a little lemon juice

Melt the syrup, butter and sugar and boil until a rich golden brown; add the Grand Marnier and about 1 teaspoon lemon juice plus a little warm water to cool the mixture. Beat the egg yolk and add to the above. Set aside to cool again. Whisk the egg whites and cream until stiff, fold into syrup mixture and serve in pretty glasses.

Roast Cotswold Duckling with Black Cherry and Wine Sauce

For 4 people

 A 5 lb duckling, dressed

1 lb (480 g) Morello cherries or a medium tin black cherries, drained
½ cup of stock (made from the duck giblets)
1 clove of garlic
½ cup red wine
a little oil
salt and pepper
1 medium onion

Rub the duck well with salt, pepper and the clove of garlic. Make 8 small slits in the breast to allow the surplus fat to run out easily. Roast in the oven with a small amount of oil at Gas Mark 6 (400°F/200°C) for about 1 hour and 15 minutes, or until duck is well done and crisp. While the duck is cooking make the sauce. Dice the onion finely and cook it in a little oil until transparent. Pour in the wine and most of the stock. If using fresh cherries add them, with the stones removed. Season to taste and simmer gently, until the liquid reduces. If you are using tinned cherries, don't add these until the stock has reduced. Remove the duck from the oven and cut it into four pieces; pour the sauce over each piece before serving. If the fresh cherries are tart, the addition of a little honey to the sauce would be delicious.

BEAR HOTEL AND RESTAURANT (B, C)

Charnham Street, Hungerford, Berkshire
Tel: Hungerford 2512 and 2062
Open 12 noon to 2 pm; 7 pm to 10 pm

If you are travelling west along the London/Bath road, you can't miss the Bear at Hungerford. Just as the A4 sweeps round to the right, there is the inn on the left-hand corner, a long, handsome, grey-painted building with the insignia of a Bear and the coat of arms of the Earls of Warwick over the front porch.

There's been an inn here since around 1300, and it came under royal patronage in Henry VIII's days when the King gave it first to Anne of Cleves, and finally to the wife who out-lived him, Katherine Parr. Elizabeth I stayed here, on one of her famous Progresses round the country. Charles I, second Stuart King of England, made it his head-quarters before the second battle of Newbury in 1643. By an ironic twist of history, Dutch William, Prince of Orange, also lodged here – in

1688 when he came to negotiate terms for the abdication of the last Stuart monarch, James II.

The Bear is built in a square, overlooking a centre courtyard. Inside, spacious rooms with log fires and beams are comfortably furnished. As well as meals in the restaurant, there are bar snacks for travellers or residents. Menus often feature English dishes, including trout pulled from the local river Kennet, joints of beef cut from loins bought in Newbury and local crayfish. Though you don't see crayfish all that often in England they are still fished from the river Dun, behind the Bear, and were popular in the seventeenth-century, when Samuel Pepys stayed at the Bear and wrote in his Diary that he had dined here 'where there are very good trouts, eels and crayfish . . .'

RECIPE FROM THE BEAR HOTEL

Celery or Asparagus Flan

This makes a delicious savoury starter.
For 4 people

The pastry:
4 oz (120 g/1 cup) flour
2 oz (60 g/4 tablespoons) butter
pinch of salt
water to mix

The filling:
1 oz (30 g/2 tablespoons) butter
2 eggs
4 stalks celery or asparagus
8 oz (240 g) cottage cheese
2 tablespoons milk
4 oz (120 g) blue Wensleydale or Blue Dorset cheese
salt and freshly ground black pepper

Make the pastry by working the butter into the flour and salt, bind into a paste with the cold water, roll out and line a flan tin. Prick the bottom and cover with a round of greaseproof paper, fill with baking beans and bake for 15 minutes at Gas Mark 6 (400°F/200°C). Remove beans and paper and leave for 3–4 minutes for centre to dry. Make the filling. Melt

118

the butter and add to it the thinly sliced celery or asparagus, cook till soft, but not brown. Place the cottage cheese in a bowl, beat in the eggs and add milk. Mash the Wensleydale with a fork and add to mixture with the celery or asparagus. Season well, put into partly cooked flan case and cook at Gas Mark 6 for about 20 minutes, until slightly brown and puffy.

THE BELL INN (B)

Long Hanborough, Oxfordshire
Tel: Freeland 881324
Open 6.45 pm to midnight (last orders 9.30 pm)

To eat at The Bell – especially on a Saturday night – you must be there by opening time. You can't book, so it's a question of first come first served. The system is simple and efficient: at the bar you collect a disc with a number; as your number is called you are given a menu and a pad and pencil and fill in your own order. When you are called to the dining room the first course is ready on the table.

The atmosphere is reminiscent of a college dining room with long refectory tables, an impression which gains substance from the number of Oxford undergraduates sharing your table. The reasonable prices, the size of the portions and the easygoing cheerfulness of it all make this the ideal meeting place for young people, though generation gaps seemed to be bridged happily in the two packed bars.

The menu offers plenty of choice and there is a good wine list. Country wines by the glass are available at the bar, apple and gooseberry as well as mead. You will find the drinks as reasonably priced as the food – a rare experience in these days of inflation!

RECIPE FROM THE BELL INN

Oxfordshire Pâté

For about 12 people
¾ lb (360 g) pig's liver
2 lb (960 g) belly of pork
4 oz (120 g) onions
1 egg beaten with 1 oz (30 g/¼ cup) plain flour

a little red wine
a little butter for cooking
salt and freshly ground black pepper
a pinch of nutmeg
1 bay leaf
1 crushed clove of garlic

Chop the liver and the pork finely. Fry the sliced onions in the butter, then add a little wine to the pan, heat quickly and add to meat mixture with seasonings and the egg beaten with the flour. Put in a terrine dish. Bake in the oven at Gas Mark 4 (350°F/180°C) for about 1½ hours with the dish standing in a baking tray of hot water. Leave to cool, then put a heavy weight on it until the next day.

THE COPPER INN (B)

Church Road, Pangbourne, Berkshire
Tel: Pangbourne 2244
Open 12.30 pm to 2.15 pm; 7.30 pm to 9.30 pm

The Thames flows majestically west from London through to Hampton Court, seat of Cardinal Wolsey, on to Windsor and the Queen's fairy-tale Castle, under a fourteenth-century stone bridge at Henley and up to Pangbourne. From here to Wallingford are some of the prettiest, less-frequented stretches of the Thames, perfect for pottering in small boats which you can hire at the water's edge. Kenneth Graham, author of *The Wind in the Willows*, lived in Church Cottage, Pangbourne and drew his inspiration from this part of the river.

The Copper Inn, rechristened thus in 1963, was built in Pangbourne in the early 1800s from ships' timbers – possibly those of Nelson's flagship, *The Elephant*, since this was the original name for the Inn, and we know that Nelson's bo'sun lived in the area.

Today, it is a very comfortable hotel; every bedroom has its own bathroom, and the large restaurant overlooks a charming garden at the back of the building. Since Tony Hampton took over the Copper Inn in 1973, the restaurant has built up a high reputation. Menus specialise in local foods – fresh fish, meat and vegetables – with game in season a speciality. The emphasis is on English dishes, often using good, old-fashioned favourites in a rather unusual way, like the recipe below for *cold* steak and kidney pie.

RECIPE FROM THE COPPER INN

Cold Steak and Kidney Pie

For this delicious variation on steak and kidney pie you need a decorated raised pie mould, or failing that a deep baking tin with a removable bottom. To give the aspic jelly enough time to set, make the pie the day before it's needed.

For 8 people

The pastry:
7 oz (210 g/14 tablespoons) butter
12 oz (360 g/3 cups) plain flour
a little more water than you would normally use for short pastry
1 beaten egg for brushing pastry

The filling:
2½ lb (1·200 kg) lean beef – topside is best
¾ lb (360 g) ox kidney
1 lb (480 g) thinly-sliced pork fat
chopped parsley
Worcester sauce
salt and pepper
aspic jelly

Make the pastry by rubbing the butter into the flour until the mixture resembles breadcrumbs, add cold water to mix. Leave enough pastry to make a lid, roll out the remainder and line the mould or tin. If using a mould work the pastry with your fingers into the moulding, taking care that it does not break. Cut the meat and the pork fat into very thin flat slices about 3 inches (76 mm) square. Put a slice of beef on a slice of pork, place a slice of kidney in the middle of the beef and roll up. Prepare the rest of the beef, pork and kidney in the same way. Fill the pie dish with the prepared rolls. Sprinkle each layer with chopped parsley, a few shakes of Worcester sauce, salt and pepper. When the pie is full, top up with water or cold beef stock. Roll out the remainder of the pastry and place on top of the pie, seal edges with beaten egg. Decorate the top, brush well with the egg wash and leave in the refrigerator for about 2 hours to rest. Then brush again with egg and bake for about 2 hours in a moderate oven, Gas Mark 4 (350°F/180°C). Cover top if pastry is getting too brown. Remove from oven, let it cool and fill with aspic jelly. It will take about ½ pint (0.28 litres/1⅓ cups). Refrigerate till set.

THE SPREAD EAGLE HOTEL (B)

Cornmarket, Thame, Oxfordshire
Tel: Thame 3661
Open 12.30 pm to 2 pm, 7 pm to 9.30 pm (9 pm Sundays)
Closed Monday lunch

Part of the Spread Eagle dates back to the sixteenth century; Charles II is supposed to have stayed here, and French prisoners are said to have been housed in the hotel's vast cellars during the Napoleonic Wars. But the hotel really found fame in the 1920s when an eccentric called John Fothergill bought it. He quickly antagonised local farmers, who had been the best customers, put an end to the regular freemasons' dinners, and made a point of showing commercial travellers that he disliked them. But his social connections plus rumours of his eccentricity attracted a new, distinguished clientele. Famous politicians, Oxford Dons and artists like Augustus John came to eat and to stay. His cooking was excellent; he boasted that they used only the best ingredients – 'of English things we have daily from three bakers three different kinds of bread made from flours that I have forced upon them, besides the breads we make ourselves, cheese from East Harptree, salt from Maldon, mustard from Leighton Buzzard, sausages – after a search all over England – from Glenthorn in Thame . . .'

Though you are no longer asked to take off your shoes and write your name on the wall, and then awarded a free meal if you are extra tall, as in John Fothergill's days, you can be sure of enjoying your visit to the Spread Eagle. Thame is a charming English country town, and the hotel is most comfortable. Bedrooms are prettily furnished and you eat in a pleasant restaurant with a relaxed atmosphere. The standard of cooking is consistently good, and the menu features a different English dish each day.

RECIPES FROM THE SPREAD EAGLE HOTEL

Autumn Pork

For 6 people
> *Half a leg of pork (the fillet end) boned*
> *1–2 carrots, finely sliced*
> *1 large onion, finely sliced*
> *1 dessertspoon salt*
> *a little fat*
> *a little corn oil*
> *1½ cups dry white wine*
> *a little cornflour*
> *½ pint (0·28 litres/1⅓ cups) good chicken stock*

The marinade:
> *½ pint (0·28 litres/1⅓ cups) dry white wine*
> *¼ pint (1·5 decilitres/⅔ cup) wine vinegar*
> *4 tablespoons olive oil*
> *3 cloves of garlic crushed*
> *1 large carrot thinly sliced*
> *2 small onions, thinly sliced*
> *10 peppercorns*
> *2 bay leaves*
> *1 sprig fresh thyme*

Rub the salt into the pork, mix the ingredients for the marinade in a bowl and turn the meat in it a few times, making sure a good amount soaks into any cracks. Then leave the meat in the covered bowl for about 2 days, turning and basting it a few times a day. Before cooking scrape off the marinade (reserve it) and drain the meat for a while before drying it gently with kitchen paper. Roll and tie the meat securely and brown it in a little hot fat. Soften the carrots and onion over a low heat in a very little corn oil, lay the meat on this and pour over 1 cup of wine and a few spoonfuls of the marinade. Cover and cook at Gas Mark 3 (325°F/170°C) for about 3 hours, or longer for a larger joint, checking and basting from time to time. Remove meat from the casserole and place it on a shallow heatproof dish or a carving tray in the oven at Gas Mark 7 or 8 (425–450°F/220–230°C) and let it brown for 15–20 minutes. Strain off excess fat and add a cream made of the cornflour mixed with the remaining white wine, blend with the meat juices, boil and stir over a low heat, adding as much of the chicken stock as you need and reducing again until a light sauce consistency is attained. Slice meat and lay evenly in a large serving dish, trickle some of the sauce over it and serve remainder in a sauceboat. Serve with apple sauce and/or a side sauce made with a crumbled slice or two of granary bread, half a large onion finely chopped and fried in butter, simmered with ½ pint (0·28 litres/1⅓ cups) of milk and blended to a thick cream with several leaves of fresh sage.

Thame Tart

From John Fothergill's own cookery book comes this description of a delicious traditional tart:
'Neither I nor Thame nor the late Lady Jekyll (in her delightful kitchen essays) invented this tart, but since tens of thousands of people have eaten it with me as "Thame Tart" it would seem to have earned the title. It's simple but stimulating; spread a short pastry flan with raspberry jam, then a layer of lemon curd and cover with whipped cream ...'
Here are more precise instructions:

For 6–8 people
  6 oz (180 g/1¼ cups) plain or self-raising flour
  pinch of salt
  3 oz (90 g/6 tablespoons) butter or margarine
  1½ teaspoonfuls caster sugar
  1 large egg yolk
  cold water to mix

The filling:
  1 or 2 tablespoons of raspberry jam
  1 or 2 tablespoons of lemon curd
  ½ pint (0·28 litres/1⅓ cups) of whipping cream

Make the pastry by rubbing the fat into the flour and salt, stir in the sugar and bind to a paste with the egg and water. Leave it to chill then roll it out and line a flan tin. Prick the base and cover it with greaseproof paper and beans to stop it rising. Bake it blind at Gas Mark 5 (375°F/190°C) for 20–30 minutes or until it's golden, removing beans and paper to let the base cook in the last 5 or 10 minutes. Allow to cool, then put a layer of raspberry jam in the bottom, smooth well and cover it with a layer of lemon curd. Whip the cream (if you like with a little caster sugar) and cover the top of the tart with it.

EAST ANGLIA
Cambridgeshire, Essex, Norfolk, Suffolk

Wm. SCRAGG'S (B, C)
2 North Hill, Colchester, Essex
Tel: Colchester 41111
Open 12 noon to 2.15 pm; 7 pm to 10.30 pm
Closed Sundays

Colchester was an important Roman town in the days when Britain was a colony, and we have to thank Caesar's legions for laying down the broad streets and straight approach roads. No wonder the Romans thought Colchester was vital, for whether you are coming from south or west, it is the natural gateway to the east coast. The Victorian resorts of Clacton and Frinton on the coast nearby are still popular at holiday time and there are several river estuaries with delightful ports where you can enjoy safe summer sailing, lovely country walks and excellent bird watching.

Over the centuries, Colchester has thriven and grown and many different forms of architecture have left their mark. The castle at the top of the town is Norman; there are timbered Tudor mansions, smart Georgian town houses, Regency bow-fronts and early Victorian workmen's cottages. North Hill, near the station, has its fair share of period exteriors, including William Scragg's, which was named after a journeyman bricklayer who lived here in the last century. This is now a seafood restaurant, run as a family business by John Thorogood.

The chef and manageress, Alice Percival, has a fine repertoire of fish dishes which vary according to the time of year. The secret of her recipes is generally fiercely guarded and her specials – such as the fish mousse – go on holiday with her! We ate at William Scragg's in March and chose from such delicacies on the winter menu as Tomato and Crab Soufflé, Mussels cooked in Cream and Wine Sauce and Smoked Trout Pâté. There were nine main courses, including Salmon cutlet with shrimp and lemon sauce, Scampi Gougère and a delicious lemon sole in a pastry case.

Colchester is famous for its oysters, 'Colchester Natives', which you can get at William Scragg's when in season. Puddings are kept deliberately light – home-made ice cream and water ices, apricot brûlé and apple charlotte were on our menu. A narrow entrance behind glass panes brings you into a friendly bar with old oak beams and a low ceiling. At lunchtime you can eat seafood snacks here, the popular fish pie for which we give you the recipe and some of the starters from the main menu with a glass of wine or real Abbott's Ale.

The dining room is in two sections. One is at the rear of the house, through the bar. This room has been very well converted with no pretence at being old, using pale pine. The other is upstairs where the seventeenth-century timbers, including the roof timbers, have been completely exposed to make a delightful dining area.

RECIPES FROM Wm. SCRAGG'S

Fish Pie

For 4 people
>   4 oz (120 g/ 8 tablespoons) butter or margarine
>   1 onion chopped
>   2 oz (60 g) mushrooms, sliced
>   3 oz (90 g/¾ cup) plain flour
>   ¾ pint (0·42 litres/2 cups) milk
>   12 oz (360 g) coley or other white fish
>   4 tomatoes, peeled, de-seeded and roughly chopped
>   pinch of mace
>   1 bay leaf
>   2 peppercorns
>   a little grated cheese
>   mashed potato to cover

Poach the fish in the milk with the peppercorns and bay leaf for about 20 minutes in a warm oven, Gas Mark 3 (325°F/160°C) until cooked. Remove the fish from the milk (keep the milk) and flake it. Gently sweat the onion in the butter or margarine until soft. Make a blond roux with the flour and add the milk to make a sauce thick enough to coat the back of the spoon. Add the sliced mushrooms and tomatoes. Season with mace, salt and freshly ground black pepper and cook for another two or three minutes. At the last minute, add the flaked fish, top with piped mashed potato and sprinkle with grated cheese. Brown under the grill and serve garnished with chopped parsley.

Smoked Trout Pâté

For 4 people
1 lb (480 g) smoked trout (or smoked mackerel)
2 oz (60 g/¼ cup) cream cheese
⅛ pint (0·75 decilitres/⅓ cup) double cream
1 tablespoon horseradish sauce
½ tablespoon freshly ground black pepper
¼ tablespoon chopped parsley
juice of half a lemon

This is a delicious pâté, but as smoked trout is expensive we have also tried it with smoked mackerel and found it very good. Skin and bone the smoked fish, place it in the blender with the cream cheese, cream, horseradish sauce, pepper, parsley and lemon juice. Blend until smooth and chill in individual pots. Serve topped with a round of lemon, with brown bread and butter.

LE TALBOOTH (C)

Gun Hill, Dedham, Essex
Tel: Colchester 323150
Open 12.30 pm to 2 pm; 7.30 pm to 9 pm all the year round

East Anglia is painter country. Gainsborough lived in the bustling small town of Sudbury; a little further east you are in the heart of Constable country – a quiet landscape which has changed very little since he painted it. Timbered houses snuggle in the folds of green hills; stately trees are mirrored in the waters of the River Stour and pretty villages vie with each other in picturesque charm. Dedham is one of the most attractive and boasts one of the best restaurants in this part of England. Le Talbooth has maintained its reputation for excellent food and service for over 20 years – a long time in a notoriously changeable trade.

The beautiful house dates back to the early 16th century, but the name may have been coined in the 18th century, from the fact that tolls were collected nearby where the Ipswich road crossed the River Stour into Suffolk. The house stands in lovely grounds along the banks of the

Stour. Constable painted it: the original is in the National Gallery of Scotland, but you can see a copy of it in the hall of the restaurant.

Half a mile away from the restaurant is Maison Talbooth, a charming Victorian house overlooking Dedham Vale and offering the comfort and luxury of a country house rather than a hotel. A lovely place to stay for exploring one of the most rewarding counties in England.

From the Talbooth menu we chose recipes for a starter – Herrings and Cream Cheese – and a fresh and delicious Iced Orange Soufflé.

RECIPES FROM LE TALBOOTH

Herrings and Cream Cheese

For 6 people
3 fresh herrings
½ pint (0·28 litres/1¼ cups) olive oil
¼ pint (1·5 decilitres/⅔ cup) vinegar
¼ pint (1·5 decilitres/⅔ cup) white wine
2 bay leaves
peppercorns
salt and pepper
6 dessert apples

For the sauce:
4 oz (120 g/1 cup) cream cheese
⅛ pint (0·75 decilitres/⅓ cup) mayonnaise
⅛ pint (0·75 decilitres/⅓ cup) double cream
chopped chives

This is an unusual and delicious starter. To make it, first marinate the cleaned, filleted and skinned herrings in the oil, vinegar and wine with the bay leaves and seasonings for 48 hours. This is almost the equivalent of cooking and there is no raw fish taste. Just before serving, drain the fish, peel and grate the apples, allowing one per person, and put apple in the bottom of the individual serving dishes. Place fish on top, half a herring per serving. Then make the sauce by mixing the cream cheese with the cream and mayonnaise, pour over the fish and add the chopped chives.

Iced Orange Soufflé

For 8 people
   3 large eggs
   6 oz (180 g / ¾ cup) sugar
   3 large oranges
   ½ pint (0·28 litres / 1¼ cups) double cream
   ½ pint (0·28 litres) vanilla ice cream

Separate the eggs, mix the yolks with the sugar and the grated zest from two of the oranges. Heat the juice of the three oranges and add to the sugar and egg mixture. Whisk the cream and add to mixture; beat in the ice cream and the whites of egg whisked to form peaks. Pour into individual glasses or bowls and chill in the freezer or the freezing compartment of the refrigerator. Serve topped with a thin orange slice.

THE WHITE HART (C)

Great Yeldham, Essex
Tel: Gt Yeldham 250
Open every day during licensing hours
Restaurant opens at 12.30 pm for lunch and 7.30 pm for dinner.

In a part of England particularly rich in old houses, the White Hart still manages to be outstanding. This black and white half-timbered building, with original Tudor chimney stacks, was completed in the reign of Henry VIII. Set back from the road, with beautifully kept gardens, it has been a hostelry for three centuries (the first application to sell ale was endorsed by the diarist Samuel Pepys). Tastefully modernised inside to add to its comfort, it retains all its original charm.

The dining room is particularly attractive, with old panelling, beamed ceiling and an open log fire in winter. The tables are set discreetly apart with candles in silver candlesticks on each and flowers from the garden – which also supplies fresh herbs and some of the vegetables. The bar is in a large and comfortable lounge where you can study the menu over a drink. At lunch time the bar snacks are very popular, including home-made soup and pâtés and a hot dish of the day in winter and a cold buffet of joints and salads in the summer.

The menu, though not overpoweringly large, offers plenty of choice, including seasonal local game and fish – the herrings we had, for which we give the simple recipe, had been caught that morning. Galantine, very popular at Elizabethan banqueting tables, is still made in the traditional way, while the crushed brandy meringues were the inventive result of having too many meringues left over after Christmas. On Saturday nights the chef is in the restaurant presiding over the trolley to carve the joint of the day – on Saturday this is always something rather special, like Beef Wellington or stuffed duck *en croûte*.

RECIPES FROM THE WHITE HART

Herrings in Butter

This simple but delicious recipe calls for very fresh fish and must be made with wholemeal flour as it gives a lovely nutty flavour to the herrings.

Allow one herring per person as a starter, two for a main course. Split open the fish, remove the backbone and retain the roe. Dredge each fish with wholemeal flour seasoned with salt and freshly milled black pepper. Fry in foaming butter, to which you have added a little lemon juice, for a few minutes together with the roe. Before serving, replace roe in the herring, serve with the hot butter, a slice of lemon and a little cold tartar sauce.

Crushed Brandy Meringues

This is a very good instant pudding and a wonderful way to use up broken meringues.

For 6 people
   1 pint (0·57 litres/2⅔ cups) double cream
   2 oz (60 g/½ cup) caster sugar (optional, the meringues are
      sweet in themselves)
   6 large meringues
   2 tots of brandy

Whip the cream and sugar, if you are using it, until the mixture stands up in peaks; break the meringues into small pieces and add to the cream, folding them in gently with the brandy. Put in the fridge for about half an hour or so. If you prepare it immediately before you start your meal, you will find it has just chilled enough when you are ready to eat it.

HINTLESHAM HALL (C)

Hintlesham, Suffolk
Tel: Hintlesham 268/227
Open 12.30 pm to 2.30 pm (last orders)
7.30 pm to 10.30 pm (last orders)

You see Hintlesham Hall before you turn into the long tree-lined drive. At night, it is a spectacular sight, with every window lit up and flood-lights bringing out the honey colour of the 18th century façade. The large and handsome house reflects the personality of its colourful owner, internationally known restaurateur Robert Carrier.

Pre-dinner drinks are served in the red and green drawing rooms – lofty rooms with fires burning in the period fireplaces, deep armchairs, good antiques, pictures and sculptures fostering the pleasant illusion that you are a guest in a stately home. The main dining room is beauti-fully proportioned, but for all its size and grandeur there is no loss of intimacy – subdued lights and tables set well apart lend cosiness to your particular corner.

You choose your four courses from an imaginative and rich menu – starred dishes come from Robert Carrier's famous book, *Great Dishes of the World*.* The food is absolutely delicious, impeccably served, every-

* (Sphere Books, 1967)

thing combining to give the evening the unmistakable stamp of a special occasion. The recipes we chose are a good cross-section of the inventive approach to food which characterises the Carrier touch: Terrine of Winter Vegetables, Saffron Soup, Guinea Fowl with Juniper Berries and Lemon Posset. If you can't get to Hintlesham, and we recommend you don't miss the experience, we hope you enjoy trying the recipes yourselves.

RECIPES FROM HINTLESHAM HALL

Saffron Soup with Fresh Herbs

For 4 people
  ½ lb (240 g) onions, coarsely chopped
  ½ lb (240 g) potatoes, coarsely chopped
  ¾ pint (0·42 litres/2 cups) milk
  1 chicken stock cube
  ½ level teaspoon saffron
  1 pint (0·57 litres/2⅔ cups) double cream

To garnish:
  4 lemon slices
  finely chopped fresh herbs

This is a delicious soup with a very subtle flavour. If you prefer it slightly less rich, use single cream or half the quantity of double cream and a little more milk. Combine the chopped onions and potatoes with the milk and the stock cube and cook until the potatoes are soft. Blend in the electric blender and then strain the mixture through a sieve. If you have no blender, put it through the mouli twice before sieving it. Stir in the saffron, add the cream and warm through. Serve hot garnished with a very thin slice of lemon and sprinkled with the herbs.

Terrine of Winter Vegetables

For 6 people
  1¼ lb (600 g) carrots
  1 pint (0·57 litres/2⅔ cups) chicken stock
  1 lb (480 g/4 cups) turnips
  ½ lb (240 g) frozen French beans
  1 packet frozen asparagus
  6 level tablespoons aspic powder
  6 tablespoons cream
  6 tablespoons good mayonnaise
  ¼ level teaspoon cayenne pepper
  a little lemon juice

This delicious terrine looks as good as it tastes and is very easy to make. Trim and scrape carrots and cut them lengthwise into quarters or eighths, according to size. Poach them in boiling chicken stock until just tender. Remove with a slotted spoon and cool. Trim and peel the turnips and cut into thin strips. Poach in boiling stock as for carrots. Remove and cool. Cook frozen French beans in the stock for five minutes, drain and cool. Prepare asparagus according to instructions on the packet. Then make mayonnaise aspic. Add ¾ pint (0·42 litres/2 cups) boiling water to the aspic powder and stir until completely dissolved. Add cream to aspic and blend well; add mayonnaise, cayenne pepper and lemon juice to taste and beat into aspic mixture until well blended. Strain mixture into a bowl and allow it to set in the refrigerator until quite syrupy. In the meantime, assemble the terrine. Arrange a layer of French beans over the bottom of a 2½ pint rectangular terrine mould or loaf tin. Place a layer of carrot strips (half the amount) on the beans, place turnip strips over carrots, arrange asparagus tips on turnips and top with remaining carrots. Holding vegetables gently in place with your fingertips, carefully pour syrupy mayonnaise aspic into terrine. Allow to set in refrigerator. Unmould and serve in slices with either a mustard mayonnaise (1–3 teaspoons Dijon mustard added to ½ pint (0·28 litres/1⅓ cups) homemade mayonnaise) or Cucumber Cream (finely diced and peeled half cucumber added to ½ pint (0·28 litres/1⅓ cups) whipped cream).

Guinea Fowl with Juniper Berries

For 6 people
3 guinea fowl
a little softened butter
1 Spanish onion, chopped
the juice of ½ lemon
12 juniper berries crushed
1 level teaspoon dried thyme
salt and freshly-ground black pepper

Quarter the birds, combine the softened butter with the chopped onion, lemon juice, crushed juniper berries, thyme, salt and pepper and brush the birds with this aromatic butter mixture. Leave the birds to absorb the flavour of the butter for at least 2 hours before cooking. If you have the facilities to charcoal grill, place the joints on the grid, skin side down, and grill for 10 to 15 minutes, then turn over, brush with the aromatic butter and cook for another 10 to 15 minutes or until the juices run quite clear when guinea fowl is pierced with a skewer through the thickest part of the leg. Alternatively, roast the guinea fowl. Place the joints in a heat-proof container and cook in a fairly hot oven, Gas Mark 7 (425°F/220°C) for 20 to 25 minutes, basting frequently with the aromatic butter. Test if bird is cooked by piercing thickest part of the leg with a skewer.

Mrs Moxon's Lemon Posset

For 4–6 people
1 pint (0·57 litres/2⅔ cups) double cream
the grated rind and juice of 2 lemons
¼ pint (1·5 decilitres/⅔ cup) dry white wine
sugar to taste
the whites of 3 eggs

Add the grated lemon rind to the pint of double cream and whisk until stiff. Stir in the lemon juice and dry white wine, add sugar to taste. Whisk the egg whites until they form peaks and fold into the whipped cream mixture. Serve in individual glasses or a glass serving dish.

PILGRIMS RESTAURANT (B)

Litcham Priory, Litcham, King's Lynn, Norfolk
Tel: Litcham 262
Open 7.30 pm to 12.30 am (Wednesday to Saturday)
12.30 pm to 2.30 pm (Sunday)
Closed Monday and Tuesday, but will open by arrangement

Named after the pilgrims who used the Priory as a stopping-place on their way to Walsingham, this skilfully converted restaurant in a delightful corner of Norfolk serves only freshly-prepared food using local produce.

It took Barbara and Mervyn Jones, who run it, only 14 months to turn what had been derelict cart and machine sheds into a charming room with a huge open fireplace, local bygones and old Norfolk prints. The local craftsmen who helped them to work the transformation were all asked to dinner on the opening night.

The menu, reassuringly, is not too large but full of interesting dishes. From it we chose the simple but very good Wayfarer's Steak, the Prune Ring (lovely with oodles of cream) and the luscious Priory Cream Cake.

RECIPES FROM PILGRIMS RESTAURANT

Wayfarer's Steak

For 4 people
4 entrecôte or fillet steaks
freshly ground black pepper
2 leaves fresh sage
4 sprigs fresh marjoram
3 sprigs fresh thyme
6 sprigs fresh parsley
1 finely-chopped clove of garlic (optional)
⅖ pint (2·27 decilitres/just under 1 cup) red wine

Slightly flatten the steaks. Lay them in a shallow dish and grind pepper liberally over them. Chop the herbs finely and mix them together, sprinkle them on the steaks, pressing them in lightly. Pour the wine over the meat and leave to marinate for a minimum of 3 hours before grilling. Serve with grilled button mushrooms and tomatoes.

Priory Cream Cake

For 6–8 people
one round sponge cake (8 in/203 mm is about right)
about ⅛ pint (0·7 litres/⅓ cup) strong black coffee (cooled)
between ⅛ and ¼ pint (0·7 to 0·14 litres/⅓ to ⅔ cup) sherry
½ pint (0·28 litres/1¼ cups) double cream

To decorate:
grated chocolate, chopped nuts, glacé cherries, or
crystallised violets to your taste

Place the sponge cake on the plate on which it will be served. Pour the cooled coffee over the sponge; when it is absorbed, gently turn cake over and pour over the sherry. Leave to stand for half an hour. Whip the cream to soft peaks and gently spread it over the top and sides of the moist sponge with a metal spoon. Swirl the top and decorate with one or other of the chosen decorations. If you're not weight-conscious serve with extra whipped cream!

Prune Ring

For about 8 people
1½ lb (720 g) good quality dried prunes
1½ pints (0·85 litres/4 cups) water, cold strained tea or mild coffee –
we used tea which is very good with the flavour of prunes

1 oz (30 g/3 tablespoons) gelatine
4 oz (120 g/½ cup) Demerara sugar
1 lemon
½ pint (0·28 litres/1¼ cups) double cream

Steep the prunes overnight in the liquid. Then, reserving ¼ pint for the gelatine, simmer the fruit, sugar and thinly pared rind of the lemon (add lemon juice too if you like) in the rest of the liquid until the prunes are soft and swollen. Drain and stone the prunes. Keep two whole for decoration. Blend the rest in the liquidiser and then push them through a sieve. Dissolve the gelatine in the reserved ¼ pint of liquid and mix with the sieved prunes and the cooking liquor. Pour into an oiled mould (preferably of the border type, so you get a ring) and leave to set in a cool place. When ready to serve, turn it out, decorate with whipped cream in the centre cavity and with the two whole prunes cut into four neat sections. Very good served with extra cream.

KNIGHT'S GATE HOTEL (B)

Little Walsingham, Norfolk
Tel: Walsingham 200
Open 12 noon to 2 pm (last orders)
7.30 pm to 10 pm (last orders)
Full English breakfast, traditional Sunday lunch

Anyone who thinks that Norfolk is a flat, rather bleak county should make for its north west corner. Here majestic corn fields swoop down towards the sea and you can walk for miles along vast sandy beaches bordered by dunes. It's an area of large estates – the Queen's at Sandringham is only a few miles away and the house is now open to the public at certain times of the year – and charming unspoilt villages; a cluster of flint and stone cottages round a pond, an old pub, a towering medieval church.

Little Walsingham is just such a village, but better known than most because it houses one of the most ancient shrines in England, that of Our Lady of Walsingham. Every Easter its narrow streets are thronged with thousands of pilgrims making the traditional pilgrimage.

The Knight's Gate Hotel is just across the road from the Shrine and is leased by its trustees to Mr and Mrs Parker, an ex-policeman from Lancashire and his Norfolk-born wife who used to run a pub in Norwich. Housed in what was once a row of 400-year-old cottages, this welcoming and cheerful pub has a restaurant and seven bedrooms. You feel instantly

138

at home as you walk into the bar, open to the rafters, with an oak gallery at one end, a carved bar counter at the other. You can have good bar food here, but the full menu is served in the long, low dining room. It's rather like eating in a friend's very pretty cottage – lots of beams, an open fire, old china displayed in alcoves along the wall. The food is simple, good and beautifully fresh. We had local trout, delivered the day before and cooked in butter with roast parsnips from the garden. We also had very good whitebait and a rich casserole of beef in red wine for which we give the recipe. Mrs Parker, who does most of the cooking, is very particular about vegetables, most of which they grow themselves and always cook to order.

RECIPE FROM KNIGHT'S GATE HOTEL

Beef in Red Wine

For 8 people
   3 lb (1·440 kg) chuck steak or lean stewing beef
   1 knuckle of veal
   1 pig's trotter
   3 large onions
   a little oil for frying
   ½ pint (0·28 litres/1¼ cups) red wine
   24 shallots
   24 button mushrooms
   3 cloves of garlic
   2 bay leaves
   bouquet garni
   pinch of marjoram
   1 tablespoon flour
   salt and freshly-ground black pepper
   ½–¾ pint (0·28–0·42 litres/1⅓–2 cups) beef stock

Fry the onions in the oil till brown. Fry the beef until brown all over, sprinkle with the flour and transfer to an oven-proof casserole. Add the pig's trotter and the knuckle of veal, the red wine, stock and seasonings. Cook in a moderate oven, Gas Mark 4 (350°F/180°C) for about 2½ hours or until the meat is nearly done. Half an hour before serving put in the shallots and mushrooms and cook for another half hour. Discard the knuckle and pig's trotter before serving. The recipe is improved if you marinate the meat overnight in the wine with the sliced onions and marjoram.

KING'S HEAD INN (B)

Front Street, Orford, Nr Woodbridge, Suffolk
Tel: Orford 271
Open daily from 12.30 pm to 2.15 pm, and 7 pm to 9 pm
Also for breakfasts and teas

Perched on the edge of the unspoilt Suffolk coast is the sleepy fishing village of Orford. Here, the river Alde runs into the North Sea under the watchful turrets of a castle built by Henry II, which has stood guard over Orford Ness for eight centuries. The great Tower with three turrets has survived unscathed and is open to visitors all year round. Inside, you can see where the guards slept, cooked, ate and – even – were imprisoned. If you climb to the flat roof at the very top, you are rewarded by a stunning view of the harbour, the sea and surrounding marshlands. In the centre of the village below, the church of St Bartholomew and the 13th-century King's Head lie cheek by jowl. The two are still connected by a secret passage used by smugglers in earlier, more romantic times. The 'gentlemen' were guided into Orford Ness by lanterns, strategically placed in windows, and sailed up-river to off-load their contraband.

Today, the King's Head is a family concern. Mine host is Ewan Shaw; his wife, Phyl, used to do the cooking but now runs the dining room while their son, Alistair, is the chef. The bar snacks are excellent, or you can eat a full-scale meal in the cosy dining room. The menu includes a number of good basics – steaks, fresh soles and mackerel – plus a choice of specials which change frequently and may include such delicacies as Oyster Mousse when there is an 'r' in the month. Their meat is locally killed and hung for 21 days, bread is home-baked, and the fish is fresh from the sea. There are four comfortable bedrooms, and even breakfast offers treats such as whole grilled plaice on the bone and smoked ham.

Mackerel Baked in Cider

For 4 people
    4 whole mackerel
    ¼ pint (1·5 decilitres/⅔ cup) dry cider
    ¼ pint (1·5 deci litres/⅔ cup) vinegar
    2 bay leaves
    1 finely chopped onion
    salt and freshly-ground pepper

Ask the fishmonger to clean, gut and remove the head and tail of the fish. Place in a casserole dish. Blanch the onion in a pan with the vinegar, let it reduce, then add the cider and bay leaves. Pour this over the mackerel, cover the casserole and bake in the oven, at Gas Mark 4 (350°F/180°C) for 15 to 20 minutes. You can serve the fish hot, or leave it to get cold and serve it with horseradish sauce.

Steak, Kidney and Oyster Pudding

For 4–6 people

The suet pastry:
    1 lb (480 g/4 cups) plain flour
    ½ lb (240 g) beef suet
    1 teaspoon salt
    ½ pint (0·28 litres/1¼ cups) cold water, or enough to mix to a
        soft dough

The filling:
    2 lb stewing steak (shin, flank or chuck)
    3 lambs' kidneys
    2 level tablespoons flour
    2 teaspoons salt
    2 teaspoons pepper
    2 large chopped onions
    6 tablespoons cold water
    6 teaspoons Worcester Sauce
    6 oysters

To make the pastry, sieve the flour and salt into a basin, remove all the skin from the suet and chop finely, using a little of the flour to prevent stickiness. Mix in with flour and make a well in the centre. Add water and mix to a soft dough. Roll out and line a basin with $\frac{3}{4}$ of the suet paste and retain $\frac{1}{4}$ for the top. Place oysters in the bottom, add the Worcester Sauce. Cut the steak and kidney into cubes, toss in seasoned flour, layer onions and meat mixture, pour in the cold water. Moisten pastry edges and cover with a pastry lid rolled from remaining pastry. Seal edges well. Cover with a double thickness of greased greaseproof paper or foil. Steam steadily for about $3\frac{1}{2}$ hours, replenishing boiling water if necessary.

Ginger Royal

For 4–5 people
   5 oz (150 g/1¼ cup) unbleached wheat flour
   1 whole preserved ginger, chopped
   pinch of salt
   3 oz (90 g/¾ cup) caster sugar
   2 eggs
   1 tablespoon corn syrup
   4 oz (120 g/8 tablespoons) margarine
   2 teaspoons ground ginger

The ginger sauce:
   ¼ pint (0·28 litres/1¼ cups) milk
   1 oz (30 g/¼ cup) cornflour
   1 level teaspoon ground ginger
   1 teaspoon lemon juice
   ½ teaspoon grated lemon rind
   golden syrup to sweeten
   6 tablespoons ginger wine

Cream the sugar and margarine until fluffy, add the eggs, and beat in well. Then fold in the flour and salt, add the chopped ginger, the ground ginger and the corn syrup. Line a baking tin with greased paper and put in the mixture. Bake in the oven at Gas Mark 4 (350°F/180°C) until it's set.

In the meantime make the sauce. Blend the cornflour with a little of the milk. Heat the rest of the milk, and pour it onto cornflour mixture, put back on the fire and stir until thickened, add golden syrup to taste, stir in the ginger, lemon juice and rind and the ginger wine. Serve very hot poured over hot pudding.

EIGHT BELLS INN (A, B)

Bridge Street, Saffron Walden, Essex
Tel: Saffron Walden 22790
Open 12 noon to 2.30 pm; 7.30 pm to 10.30 pm (last orders 9 pm)

Village pubs are as much a part of our English tradition as the monarchy or roast beef, and they are generally a good place to stop for a bite of lunch in warm, welcoming surroundings. But every now and then, you come across one that is outstanding, like the Eight Bells, which combines a very friendly atmosphere in Tudor surroundings with really good home-made food. Jackie Money, wife of the licensee, Elven, does most of the cooking herself and tries out new dishes on her family, or helpers in the bar, before they go up on the blackboard as part of the daily menu. There's a good choice, ranging from home-made soup and hot dish of the day to duckling pâté (flavoured with herbs and wine) and cheeses with fresh-baked bread.

At night dinner is in a lovely 15th-century 'barn', at the back of the sprawling Elizabethan pub. If there are only two of you dining, you may sit up in the little minstrels' gallery that overlooks the timbered room. It is a different menu to the lunchtime one, offering good English dishes cooked in the traditional way by the chef – 'King Henry's Beefe stake', 'Fresshe pyke with Safroun sauce' and 'Queen Anne trout' are regulars on the menu.

Saffron Walden is a pretty town, and well-placed for sight-seeing round this corner of Essex. Cambridge is only about 15 miles away, Thaxted and Finchingfield are nearer still and Audley End – a glorious house that was once a Royal Palace – is on the doorstep.

RECIPES FROM THE EIGHT BELLS

Old English Beef in Ale

This is a lovely way to cook a beef stew. The ale tenderises the meat, the port offsets the sharpness of the ale and the marjoram gives the whole thing a tangy bouquet.

For 8–10 people
  3 large onions
  6 carrots
  1 lb (480 g) mushrooms
  a large pinch of marjoram
  3 lb (1·440 kg) stewing beef
  ½ pint (0·28 litres/1¼ cup) pale ale
  2 tots of port
  enough beef stock to cover (use stock cubes)
  4–6 rashers streaky bacon
  dripping or a mixture of oil and butter for frying
  flour for thickening

Fry the bacon in dripping or oil and butter until the fat runs, add the sliced onions and the carrots cut lengthwise in thin strips, put in the mushrooms; let all the vegetables fry gently until softened and coated in fat. Fry the meat separately until well browned; combine meat and vegetables and sprinkle liberally with flour, leave this to amalgamate for a few minutes before adding the ale and port; let the mixture bubble for a minute or two then add enough hot stock just to cover the whole thing, add the marjoram, salt and freshly-milled pepper and simmer on top of the stove or in a moderate oven for about 2 hours, or until the meat is tender.

Tipsy Prawns

This simple and excellent recipe has the added merit of being very versatile. Served in individual ramekins it makes an unusual starter; for a main course it can be accompanied by rice (make the rice in a ring mould and put the hot prawns in the middle for a dinner party), or by hot mashed potato in little oven-proof dishes. If you are serving it on its own it is equally good cold.

For 4 people
  2 onions
  *1 pint (0·57 litres/2⅔ cups) single cream or half milk and half
     double cream*
  1 or 2 tablespoons flour
  a little butter
  ½ lb (240 g) peeled prawns

2 measures of whisky
a little chopped parsley for garnish

Peel and slice the onions and fry them gently in butter until softened and transparent. Add the flour and let it cook for a few minutes, then add the cream, or cream and milk, and let the sauce cook and thicken. Pour in the whisky and let it simmer for a while then add the prawns and let them cook in the sauce. Sprinkle with chopped parsley just before serving.

THE OLD VIC WINE BAR (B)

Waterloo Road, London SE1
Tel: 928 8197
Open 12 noon to 3 pm; 6 pm to 7.30 pm
Closed Sundays

Situated in the Stalls Bar of one of the most evocative theatres in London, this friendly, busy wine bar makes you wish that every theatre in London offered the same facilities.

As you go downstairs at lunchtime you are met by a reassuring combination of sounds and smells – laughter and the hubbub of voices, the chink of glasses and the smell of good coffee. You choose your food from a long counter; there are one or two hot dishes a day, like the very good steak and kidney pie for which we give the recipe, a choice of pâtés, cold roast beef and ham, a selection of imaginative salads – we liked the diced cucumber and walnuts – and a good cheese board with French bread and biscuits. The adjacent bar offers a wide choice of wine (many of them by the glass: how nice not to be met by one red, one white and a rosé) and delicious Bucks Fizz (champagne and orange juice).

The bar is attractively decorated with old theatre programmes and large areas of walls papered with photographs of actors and actresses who have played at the Vic. There is something of the atmosphere of a good club and the chance to see the cast who may be rehearsing on that day. Do book if you go at lunchtime as it gets very busy. In the evening the bar is open to ticket holders only, an hour and a half before the start of the performance.

RECIPE FROM THE OLD VIC WINE BAR

Steak and Kidney Pie

A slightly different approach to this traditional favourite – the pastry is baked separately on a baking sheet, so you get a thin crisp piece of short-crust pastry with your steak and kidney.

For 6 people

The filling:

    2 oz (60 g/¼ cup) dripping or a mixture of oil and butter
    1 large onion
    2 lb (960 g) chuck steak
    ¾ lb (360 g) ox kidney
    ¼ teaspoon garlic salt
    ¾ pint (0·42 litres/2 cups) stock
    ¼ pint (1·5 decilitres/⅔ cup) red wine
    bouquet garni
    salt and pepper

Fry the onion in half the fat, drain and leave on the side. Sear the steak in the rest of the fat, add the wine, let it bubble for a few minutes, then add the stock, garlic salt and bouquet garni. Let the mixture simmer for an hour, then add the chopped kidney and cook for about another hour, or until meat and kidney are tender. Check seasoning and thicken with *beurre manié* (little knobs of butter rolled in flour).

The pastry:

    6 oz (180 g/1½ cups) flour
    1½ oz (45 g/3 tablespoons) butter
    1½ oz (45 g/3 tablespoons) margarine
    about 2 tablespoons water
    pinch of salt

Sift the flour and salt into a bowl, rub in the fats until you get a bread-crumb consistency, and mix to a pliable paste with the water. Chill in the refrigerator for about 15 minutes, then roll out to ¼-inch thickness and bake for 20–30 minutes at Gas Mark 6 (400°F/200°C).

TURPIN'S RESTAURANT (B)

118 Heath Street, London NW3
Tel: 435 3791
Dinner from 6.30 pm to 11 pm (last orders)
Traditional Sunday lunch
Closed Sunday night and all day Monday

Eating at Turpin's is rather like dining in a very pretty private house. Half-way up Heath Street, the steep narrow road which links Hampstead Village to the Heath, you turn into a charming side garden – a knock on the door and you are in a tiny front hall from which open two small, intimate dining rooms, each with only six or seven tables. White panelling in one and forest green walls in the other look particularly evocative by candlelight and echo the eighteenth-century elegance of the house.

Like so many Hampstead houses, this one has a history. A certain Professor Sweet, a teacher of phonetics who lived here, knew Bernard Shaw and is believed to be the model for one of Shaw's most unforgettable characters – Professor Higgins in *Pygmalion*.

The menu features many English dishes and some unusual ones like the very good Cream of Brussels Sprouts Soup for which we give the recipe. Vegetables are fresh and well cooked, there is a good wine list with moderately priced house wines and the service by friendly Spanish waiters is attentive and efficient.

RECIPE FROM TURPIN'S

Cream of Brussels Sprouts Soup

For 4 people
  1 lb (480 g) sprouts
  2 oz (60 g/4 tablespoons) butter
  1 onion
  1½ pints (0·85 litres/4 cups) chicken stock
  salt and pepper

Cut sprouts in half, removing yellow or blackened leaves and wash very carefully. Chop the onion and fry it in the butter until softened, add the sprouts and leave them to simmer for a few minutes, tossing the pan so they all get covered in the butter. Add the hot stock (you can use stock cubes) and allow to cook till the sprouts are soft. Blend in the liquidiser or pass through a mouli. Add salt and pepper to taste, if too thick for your liking thin with milk or stock. Before serving add a little cream or lump of butter.

JUSTIN DE BLANK (B)

54 Duke Street, London W1
Tel: 629 3174
Open 9 am to 3.30 pm; 4.30 pm to 9.30 pm
Closed Saturday pm and all day Sunday

A haven for weary shoppers (within a stone's throw of Selfridges and Marks & Spencer) this high-class take-away/self-service restaurant has room to seat 60 at unusual cane benches and zinc-topped tables with a view of white walls and indoor plants.

The varied menu changes daily and includes home-made soups and pâtés, a choice of hot dishes, salads and cold food and an array of tempting puddings, like the Fruit Brûlée for which we pass on the recipe.

Good coffee, wines by the glass or bottle and a choice of non-alcoholic drinks including Suffolk apple juice comp ete the menu. It's not really cheap, but very good quality and large helpings.

RECIPE FROM JUSTIN DE BLANK

Fruit Brûlée

This is one combination of fruit used for this delicious alternative to fruit salad, but you can work out your own variations according to the season.

For 4–6 people
1 ripe banana
1 mandarin orange or satsuma
1 comice pear
½ small fairly firm pineapple
1 Chinese gooseberry
¼ lb (120 g) small strawberries
¼ lb (120 g) Muscat grapes
4 oz (120 g/¾ cup) Demerara sugar (the recipe specifies
  Caribbean, not London Demerara)
½ gill (0·75 decilitres/⅓ cup) orange juice including a tablespoon
  lemon juice
½ gill (0·75 decilitres/⅓ cup) brandy (optional)
¾ pint (0·42 litres/2 cups) double cream

Slice the banana, the Chinese gooseberry and the pear into $\frac{1}{4}$-inch pieces; cut the pineapple into small chunks; section the mandarin orange; halve and seed the grapes; leave the strawberries whole. Place all fruit into a shallow oven-proof dish. Pour over the orange juice and brandy. Whisk the cream until firmly whipped and spread over the fruit. Chill the whole dish for at least two hours. Then sprinkle with the sugar and place under a very hot grill until the sugar caramelises with the cream. If the dish won't fit under the grill, an acceptable substitute is to pour caramel, still bubbling, over the chilled fruit and cream.

THE RED LION (C)

1 Waverton Street, Mayfair, London W1
Tel: 499 1307
Open 12 noon to 3 pm (last orders 2 pm); 7 pm to 10.30 pm
(last orders 9.45 pm)
Closed Sunday evening

This handsome pub/restaurant used to be part of a farmhouse in the days when Mayfair was a village. Prestige office blocks, towering hotels and pretty houses now surround it instead of fields, but inside perfectly preserved is the welcoming atmosphere of an English inn with exposed beams, fine panelling and shining brass and copper.

The Red Lion is in a cul-de-sac which provides a pretty paved area for outdoor drinking on summer evenings. Off the bar is the small restaurant, impeccably run – snowy starched tablecloths, flower-filled windows, attractive china and discreet service.

The set lunch menu is very good value with a choice of carefully cooked English dishes – the ideal place to bring overseas businessmen. Dinner is more elaborate, with a fuller à la carte menu and an intimate atmosphere. There are only a few tables, so it is essential to book. Salads and hot snacks are available in the bars at lunchtime.

RECIPE FROM THE RED LION

Poached Halibut in Prawn Sauce

For 4 people
   4 fillets of halibut

1 onion
2 carrots
bouquet garni
salt and pepper
1 cup white wine
dash of Tabasco sauce
¼ pint (0·28 litres/1⅓ cup) milk
1 oz (30 g/2 tablespoons) butter
1 oz (30 g/¼ cup) flour
1 cup dry white wine
4 oz (120 g) peeled prawns
2 tablespoons double cream

First make a court bouillon for poaching the fish with 3 pints of water, the onion, carrots, bouquet garni and a cup of white wine (or a couple of tablespoons of wine vinegar). Season with salt and pepper and a dash of Tabasco, bring to the boil then let it simmer for 35–45 minutes. Poach the halibut in the court bouillon very slowly for about 15 minutes. To make the sauce: make a bechamel sauce with the flour, butter and the milk (or use half milk, half court bouillon); add to it a cup of dry white wine and let it reduce rapidly; add the peeled prawns, the double cream and pour over the halibut. Serve at once. You can use this method of cooking for turbot, or haddock fillets.

THE TATE GALLERY RESTAURANT (C)

Millbank, London SW1
Tel: 834 6754
Open 12 noon to 3 pm daily except Sunday

Among the many museums and art galleries London has to offer, it's interesting to find one which can be recommended for its cuisine as well as its collection! The Tate Gallery Restaurant – open for lunch Monday to Saturday – serves a wide variety of excellent English food, some of it faithfully reproduced from carefully researched recipes of centuries ago.

As well as a regular menu of starters, hot grills, cold buffet and sweets there is a selection of dishes that changes once a week, including roast joints, poultry and fish in season.

The dining room, once known as the Whistler Room because of the

Whistler murals, is light and spacious with modern tables and chairs. The waitresses, dressed in black like their Victorian counterparts, offer a smiling service and the wine list is exceptional both for choice and value. We chose from the regular menu one of Queen Elizabeth I's favourite meat dishes – Veal Kidneys Florentine, cooked with fresh spinach in sherry; and Mrs Joan Cromwell's Grand Sallet, a mixture of green beans, nuts, olives and dried fruits bound with cream. The recipe comes from a book published in 1664 which begins with an anti-Cromwell essay referring to 'the Wife of the Late Userper, Truly described and represented' before revealing Mrs Cromwell's culinary secrets.

RECIPES FROM THE TATE GALLERY

Elizabethan Veal Kidneys Florentine

If you can't get veal kidneys you can make this with lamb's kidneys, though the veal has a more delicate flavour. A sixteenth-century recipe calls for a rich, short pastry, laid in a shallow, buttered platter with the filling heaped in the middle and another piece of pastry on the top. A recipe from 1605 uses puff pastry; for today's cooks we suggest using ready-made frozen vol-au-vent cases, baked, and filled with the mixture just before serving.

For 4 people

   3 veal or lamb kidneys or 1½ lb (720 g) (whichever is greater)
   1 lb (480 g) fresh spinach (use frozen if you must)
   ¼ cup sherry or port
   flour
   ground mace
   sugar to taste
   6 oz (180 g/1¼ cup) dried mixed fruit
   ¾ pint (0·42 litres/⅔ cups) veal stock
   salt and pepper
   veal dripping or a mixture of oil and butter
   7¼ oz (218 g) short rich pastry or 12 frozen vol-au-vent cases

Clean and roughly chop the kidneys and sauté them in the dripping or oil and butter until golden brown; add the sherry or port and the veal stock, thicken with a little flour and cook for a few minutes. Add the dried fruit (the more you use the sweeter it will be, so taste as you add small amounts; the Elizabethans also added sugar). Season with salt, pepper and a little mace. Cook until the fruit is soft and then add the cooked and well-drained spinach. Keep hot until the vol-au-vent cases are ready for filling.

'Grand Sallet'

The unusual combination of flavours produces a rich mixture – a small amount would make an unusual starter – but it is a very good way to use up leftover chicken. Cromwell's wife used shrimps or cooked sturgeon as an alternative to chicken. Good as a summer buffet dish.

For 6–8 people

   3 oz (90 g/¾ cup) raisins
   1–2 oz (30 to 60 g/⅓ to ⅔ cup) capers
   2 oz (60 g/⅓ cup) pickled cucumbers
   grated rind of 1 lemon
   3 oz (90 g/ ¾ cup) blanched and flaked almonds
   2 oz (60 g/ ⅓ cup) black olives
   about ¼ pint (1·5 decilitres/⅔ cup) single cream acidulated with the
      juice of half a lemon
   1½ lb (720 g) cooked haricots verts *coarsely chopped*
   for the main ingredient use 12 oz (360 g/2⅔ cups) of shelled
      shrimps or chopped cooked chicken

Simply mix all the ingredients together and serve in a salad bowl or dish; the seventeenth-century original was garnished with the *haricots verts* and raw turnip, sliced and cut into patterns, the whole salad laid on a platter round an imitation tree of wax. For modern cooks, it's quite a good idea to keep the sallet in the fridge: it is very good cold on a warm day.

THE UPPER CRUST IN BELGRAVIA (B)

9 William Street, London SW1
Tel: 235 8444
Open 11.30 am to 3 pm; 6 pm to 11.30 pm, daily
Closed Christmas Day and Boxing Day

Ideally placed for shoppers in the Knightsbridge area, this cosy restaurant is quite literally a dream come true for owner Manny Franks. A butcher by training and the son of a butcher, Manny went into catering when he ran the Lowndes Cafe on these premises 27 years ago. One morning in 1973 he called in both his sons. 'Boys, I've had a dream . . . a restaurant that looks like a farmhouse and serves good traditional English food – pies, puddings, farmhouse loaves, herby butters . . .'

Well, it's all there now at the Upper Crust. Old bricks on the walls, brick floors, pine panelling, Windsor chairs, thick brown pottery . . . down to the delicious hot bread and herb butter. Pies with feather-light pastry topping are the mainstay of the menu. The fillings are inventive – Steak and Giblets; Turkey and Pimento; Turkey, Celery and Cranberry; Steak and Pickled Walnut. Yorkshire Pudding is used as a pastry case. We had it as a delicious starter, filled with chicken livers, but it's also served as a pudding, filled with mincemeat. The menu includes traditional main courses like Pickled Brisket of Beef, Baked Mackerel with Gooseberry Sauce, Boiled Ham, Roast Rack of Lamb.

The cover charge actually does cover something – the bread and herb butter and a selection of vegetables, these last bought fresh by students from local catering colleges, doing their industrial training with the company. The meat comes from the Franks family's other concern – a stylish butchers in Fulham where all the meat is British – Canterbury lamb, Scottish beef, Norfolk turkeys. There's game in season and a wonderful array of fish. It's called Wainwright and Daughter, after Mrs Franks's first boyfriend and the daughter of the family. Two other restaurants are operated by the same management – Dizzy's Diner in Knightsbridge behind Harrods and the Milk Churn in Hampstead.

The Upper Crust is open seven days a week. 'It's like a fourteen-day week', says son David Franks, who helps to run the business. Rather like doctors, the family are on call to the staff; there is always a number they can ring if there is a panic. But panics are rare in an organisation where the chef has been there for 27 years and the manageress for 24.

RECIPES FROM THE UPPER CRUST

Yorkshire Pudding filled with Chicken Livers

This works best if you make individual puddings. While the puddings are cooking sauté the chicken livers; keep them hot and when the puddings are done and nicely risen cut them in half and fill them with the liver mixture. Served piping hot they make a delicious starter, or with vegetables a good supper dish for the family.

The batter (for 12 individual puddings):
  2 oz (60 g/½ cup) flour
  pinch of salt
  1 large egg
  ¼ pint (1·5 decilitres/⅔ cup) milk – or milk and water

Mix flour and salt in a bowl, make a well in the middle and add the whole egg and a little milk. Stir in the flour gradually from the sides, stir and go on adding half the milk. Beat for about 7 minutes, stir in the rest of the milk. Or you can put all the ingredients in a liquidiser and blend them together. Cover the bowl and leave it to stand for half an hour in a cool place. Then heat a small knob of lard in 12 bun tins. When it is smoking hot half fill the tins with the batter as quickly as you can so the fat does not cool. Bake for 15–20 minutes at Gas Mark 7 (425°F/220°C).

The filling:
  8 oz (240 g) chicken livers
  1 onion, finely chopped
  a knob of butter
  1 tablespoon sherry
  salt and pepper
  mixed herbs

Sauté the onion in the butter until softened, add the livers; when they are brown, add the sherry, herbs, salt and pepper and simmer until tender. Keep warm until ready to fill puddings.

Chocolate Brandy Cream

For 6 people
½ pint (0·28 litre/1¼ cups) single cream
½ lb (240 g) plain unsweetened chocolate
1 egg
the grated rind of half an orange
1 tablespoon brandy

Heat the cream, but don't let it boil. Put the brandy, grated orange rind and the cream in the liquidiser, chop the chocolate and add it. Blend the whole thing, then add the egg and blend again. Put into ramekins and leave to set in the fridge or a cold larder. If you have no blender melt the chocolate with the brandy, add it to the hot cream, whisk it all together and then add the egg and grated rind.

DRAKES AT POND PLACE (B)

2A Pond Place, Fulham Road, London SW3
Tel: 584 4555
Open seven days a week for lunch and dinner

Set back a short distance from the bustle of the Fulham Road, Drakes is a very attractive, air-conditioned restaurant where old materials have been used most successfully to create a stylish and unmistakably twentieth-century atmosphere. The floor flags, exposed wall bricks and beams come from a Tudor barn in Hampshire; combined with warm browns and cream, soft lights and good pictures, it makes a welcoming and relaxing setting in both the restaurant and roomy bar. You can just go in for a drink in the comfortable bar, but what a pity to miss the excellent food!

The head chef, who devises most of the recipes, often using old English cookbooks for inspiration, used to be at the Savoy, as did a number of his assistants. With the manager he plans a new menu every three months to make the most of seasonal produce. When available, the menu includes suckling pig and game; very good duck (they'd have to with a name like Drakes) and spit-roasted meat joints and poultry.

Everything we tried, including crisp and fresh vegetables, was so good that we had difficulty in narrowing our selection down to three recipes. We chose Cucumber and Cream Cheese Mousse as a starter (or in larger quantities a good summer main course) for its delicate fresh flavour; Tripe and Onions in Cider because this is a nice way to cook an old English favourite and hot Treacle and Orange Tart since it literally melts in the mouth! There is no cover charge at Drakes, no minimum charge and prices include VAT which makes the food, the setting and the service some of the best value in London.

RECIPES FROM DRAKES

Cream Cheese and Cucumber Mousse

For 6 people
   12 oz (360 g/2 cups) cream cheese
   6 oz (180 g/1¼ cups) cucumber
   4 gelatine leaves or ½ oz (15 g/1½ tablespoons) powdered gelatine
   2½ tablespoons wine vinegar
   6 standard egg whites
   salt and pepper

Break up the leaf gelatine into the wine vinegar and leave to stand until completely softened. Cut the cucumber into dice but do not peel – liquidise it in the blender or, if you have no blender, grate the cucumber. Soften the cream cheese with a fork, add the cucumber to it and mix thoroughly. Melt the gelatine over hot water and add it to the cucumber mixture. Whip the egg whites to a fluffy consistency and fold into the cheese and cucumber, check seasoning and allow to set either in individual dariole moulds or in a large mould. If you want to decorate it, place very thin cucumber slices in the bottom of the mould, pour in a small amount of melted gelatine and allow to set before pouring in the mixture.

Tripe and Onions

For 4 people
   1½ lb (720 g) tripe diced to approximately 1 inch

1 lb (480 g) sliced onions
½ pint (0·28 litres/1¼ cups) dry cider
½ pint (0·28 litres/1¼ cups) brown sauce
salt and pepper
1 bay leaf
a pinch of thyme

Brown sauce:
1½ tablespoons chopped lean bacon
1 oz (30 g/⅓ cup) chopped celery
1 oz (30 g/⅓ cup) chopped onion
1 oz (30 g/⅓ cup) chopped carrot
3 tablespoons oil
2 oz (60 g/½ cup) flour
1½ pints (0·85 litres/4 cups) beef stock – use cubes
1 tablespoon tomato purée

The recipe calls for ½ pint of demi-glace sauce. This is complicated to make domestically and we suggest a good brown sauce as an alternative. To make this, first simmer the bacon for 10 minutes in water, then drain and add to the chopped celery, onion and carrot and fry all the ingredients in the hot oil. Add the flour and cook for about 10 minutes until golden brown. Whisk in the boiling beef stock and when mixed add the tomato purée. Simmer for 2 hours, removing scum from time to time. Then fry the sliced onions lightly in a little oil and butter, pour in the dry cider and brown sauce and add the tripe with the bay leaf and a pinch of thyme, bring all to the boil and skim. Simmer for about an hour, until the tripe is tender. When ready season with salt and pepper.

Hot Treacle and Orange Tart

For 4–6 people

The pastry:
4 oz (120 g/1 cup) plain flour
2 oz (60 g/4 tablespoons) butter
1 oz (30 g/2 tablespoons) sugar
1 small egg
pinch of salt

The filling:

4 oz (120 g/1 cup) crushed digestive biscuits
4 oz (120 g /¼ cup) golden syrup
zest from one orange
and the orange, sliced

Make the pastry by rubbing the butter into the flour and salt until you get a sandy texture. Mix the egg with the sugar and add to the flour, mix gently until you get a smooth paste. Leave to rest under a teacloth for at least ten minutes, then place in a flan case. Mix the crushed digestive biscuits with the golden syrup and the orange zest and place in the uncooked flan case. Place orange slices over the mixture and cook in a moderate oven, Gas Mark 6 (400°F/200°C) for about 20–25 minutes or until the pastry is cooked. Serve hot with thick cold cream.

THE HUNGRY HORSE (B)

196 Fulham Road, London SW10
Tel: 352 7757
Open 6.30 pm to midnight (last orders) Monday to Saturday
Sunday 12.30 pm to 3 pm (traditional Sunday lunch)
and 7 pm to 11 pm

It's taken an Australian owner and a Sicilian manager to produce some of the most authentic English food in London at its simple best.

This small friendly restaurant, tucked away behind a white-washed courtyard, offers traditional favourites like boiled beef and dumplings, steak, kidney and mushroom pie, salmon fish cakes and a list of puddings that would win approval from Mrs Beeton herself. There are some very good soups, particularly the Lemon Fish Soup, for which we give the recipe, served with a lovely tart egg sauce that is the Hungry Horse's own creation.

The serving dishes are left on your table and you help yourself to as much as you want. The vegetables are particularly good – hot red cabbage, very crisp white cabbage in butter and roast potatoes that are just as mother ought to make them, crisp outside and melting inside!

The site was once a bakery; now you go down a flight of steps, through a little yard green with plants and into two small rooms decorated with black and white tiles and handsome Edwardian glass and mirrors. It's nice to be served by smiling waiters who don't make you feel you're dawdling over the coffee even though space is at a premium.

From the varied menu, we chose recipes for the fish soup and boiled beef and dumplings, just to show how very good simple English food can be.

RECIPES FROM THE HUNGRY HORSE

Lemon Fish Soup

This delicious creamy soup, served with sharp (cold) egg sauce is almost a meal in itself. Serve it with hot French bread or thinly sliced brown bread and butter.

For 5–6 people
½ lb (240 g) white fish – cod, coley, or halibut if you're rich
½ lb (240 g) smoked haddock
1 onion
bouquet garni
1 chopped onion
3 oz (90 g/6 tablespoons) butter
½ pint (0·28 litres/1⅓ cups) milk
2 oz (60 g/½ cup) flour
salt and pepper
1 lemon
a little single cream

The egg sauce:
4 hard-boiled eggs
½ pint (0·28 litres/1⅓ cups) milk
3 oz (90 g/¾ cup) flour
2 oz (60 g/4 tablespoons) butter
Tabasco
Worcester sauce
anchovy essence
2 tablespoons finely chopped fresh parsley
a little single cream

Poach the fish in water with an onion and the bouquet garni. When fish is cooked, take it out of the stock (keep this), remove any bones and flake the fish. Chop an onion finely and soften it in half the butter; while it's colouring, make a white sauce with flour, rest of butter and ½ pint of milk. Add the fish stock and white sauce to the softened onion, let it boil. Then add the cod and haddock, check seasoning, add the juice of half a lemon and just before serving add a little cream.

Make the Egg Sauce in advance. Hard boil the eggs and chop them up. Make a thick sauce with ½ pint of milk, flour and butter, add as much of the sauce as you need to give the eggs a thick, creamy consistency. Now add the Worcester sauce, anchovy essence and Tabasco, a teaspoon at a time until you have a flavour you like. Be particularly careful with the Tabasco which is very hot. Squeeze in a little lemon juice, add the chopped parsley and pour in a dash of cream. Serve cold in a bowl to accompany the soup.

Boiled Beef and Dumplings

This traditional English dish is equally good hot or cold, so it's worth making it in a large piece.

For 10–12 people
  4–5 lb (1·92 to 2·40 kg) silverside
  1 large onion
  a couple of leeks
  3 carrots
  half a dozen whole black peppercorns
  1 glass red wine or cider

Soak the silverside for about 4 hours in cold water. Drain it and put it in a saucepan or casserole just a little bit bigger than the joint. Pour over it the wine or cider, slice the onion, chop the leeks and add them together with the whole carrots and peppercorns. Fill the pan or casserole with water to cover the meat. Either simmer on top of the stove or cook it in a slow oven Gas Mark 2 or 3 (330°–325°F/150°–160°C) for about 4 hours or until meat is tender but not too soft or it will crumble when carving. Serve it with boiled carrots with parsley and butter and the dumplings. The stock will make a good gravy to accompany the meat.

Dumplings

  8 oz (240 g/2 cups) self-raising flour
  3 oz (90 g/⅔ cup) suet

pinch of salt, pepper, a little sage
about ¼ pint (1·5 decilitres/⅔ cup) water

Sieve the flour, salt and pepper, mix in the sage, stir in the suet and mix to a slightly soft but not sticky dough with the water. Divide into 12–18 portions, and shape them into little rounds with floured hands. Cook for about 20 minutes on top of the boiled beef.

HATHAWAYS (B)

13 Battersea Rise, London SW11
Tel: 228 3384
Open 7 pm to 10.30 pm
Closed Sundays

Behind the red front door of No. 13 Battersea Rise you will find that rare thing in England – a real family restaurant. Run by a husband and wife team, Carl and Kathie Scheiding, and called after the family cat (in turn bearing the name of a classy make of shirt because of his snowy shirt-front), it's reached the happy stage where the regulars are on first name terms.

It's pretty and intimate with red hessian on the walls, flowered table-cloths, fresh flowers on the tables and a trolley bearing a good selection of cheese and home-made puddings.

You wait for a little for your order but who cares when it means it's freshly cooked and you're brought a bowl of salad with an unusual yog-hurt and nut dressing to fill the gap? Everything except the ice cream is made on the premises – it's simple, good and excellent value. Kathie Scheiding is Canadian and includes some Transatlantic touches in her basically English recipes, like the addition of sweetcorn to the very good chicken and mussel pie. Her marinated mutton was particularly mem-orable – the wine sauce giving it a gamey flavour – a lovely way to cook a traditional English meat, now almost dying out, ousted by the demand for lamb. We give you the recipe for this and the chocolate and cherry trifle, deliciously creamy without being too rich. Excellent coffee and a good house wine from an interesting wine list completed an inexpen-sive and well-served meal. Do book: it's small as well as popular.

Marinated Mutton

For 8–10 people
  half a leg of mutton (weighing about 4 lb/1·92 kg)
  2 onions, peeled and sliced
  3 carrots peeled and cut into chunks
  2 leeks, trimmed, washed and cut into pieces
  2 cloves of garlic finely chopped
  sprig of fresh parsley
  2 tablespoons mixed herbs
  2 tablespoons salt
  10 whole peppercorns and 4 whole cloves
  ½ bottle dry red wine
  ½ gill (0·75 decilitres/⅓ cup) white wine vinegar
  2 tablespoons Demerara sugar
  2 bay leaves
  ¼ pint (1·5 decilitres/⅔ cup) vegetable or olive oil

Get the butcher to bone the joint for you, trim off the fat and tie it in a neat shape. Combine the carrots, onions, leek and garlic and sauté them lightly in the oil. Add all the other ingredients (except the meat) and bring to the boil; simmer for a few minutes and allow to cool. Place the mutton in a container and pour the marinade over – leave in a cool place for 2 or 3 days, turning the meat a couple of times a day. When ready to cook, drain the joint well, reserving the marinade. Sear mutton on all sides in a large frying pan. Transfer to a large casserole, pour over the marinade and vegetables, cover tightly and braise in a moderate oven Gas Mark 3 or 4 (325°–350°F/160°–180°C) for about 2 hours, or until tender. When cooked, keep meat warm, drain marinade and thicken it with little knobs of butter rolled in flour. Serve sliced with the hot gravy.

Chocolate and Cherry Trifle

For 6 people
  a chocolate sponge cake (make it from a mix)
  1 small glass of dark rum (about ⅛ pint)
  A 1lb tin of Black Morello cherries pitted and drained
     (use the syrup for another pudding)
  1 pint (0·57 litre/2⅔ cups) milk plus 2 tablespoons

2 tablespoons custard powder
4 oz (120 g) plain unsweetened chocolate
whipped cream and grated chocolate for decoration

Make up the sponge cake and leave it to cool. Slice into two. Sprinkle some of the rum in a dessert dish, put half of the sponge on top and sprinkle with more rum and half the cherries. Mix 2 tablespoons of cold milk with the custard powder (it is not worth making your own custard as the rum and chocolate give the flavour to this delicious trifle). Heat the rest of the milk with the chocolate cut into pieces until the chocolate is dissolved. Gradually stir the chocolate milk into the custard mixture, return it to the heat and simmer gently stirring all the time until smooth and thick. Pour half the chocolate custard over the cake layer, then make another layer of cake, rum, cherries and custard. Leave the pudding to cool and decorate with whipped cream and grated chocolate.

THE REFECTORY (A, B)

6, Church Walk, Richmond, Surrey
Tel: 940 6264
Open 10 am to 12 noon for coffee; 12 noon to 3 pm for lunch from Tuesday to Saturday
Open for dinner on Thursday, Friday and Saturday
Open for Sunday lunch 12 noon to 3 pm
Closed all day Monday

If you can imagine having Sunday lunch with one of the nicest families you know, you have some idea of what it's like to eat at Mary and Roger Kingsley's highly personal restaurant.

Helped by their sixth child, who is currently training in their kitchen, Mary does most of the cooking. 'We don't use tinned or convenience foods,' she says, 'and we try to put a bit of love and care into what we serve.'

Husband Roger welcomes you at the door and takes you to your table in an attractive dining room. Decor is simple, brown walls hung with paintings (for sale) by local artists; modern pine tables, benches and chairs. In summer, you can also eat outside in a pretty courtyard with hanging baskets of flowers, overlooking the church which has a Tudor porch and tower.

The food is served on handsome pottery dishes from spotless kitchens which were once the the lavatories of the Parish Rooms! Roger is a member of the Parochial Church Council of Richmond who decided in 1975 that the site in an eighteenth-century building should be renovated and put to good community use. The menu is exclusively British

with many regional specialities and unusual dishes – brown rice and mushrooms, potted smoked fish, Lancaster Lemon Tart to name a few. Dinner by candlelight includes some of the lunchtime menu, but is a touch more sophisticated. The restaurant is licensed and Roger Kingsley's selection of medium-priced English-grown and made grape wines and country wines made with berries will surprise those who have no faith in English wines.

RECIPES FROM THE REFECTORY

Cidered Pork, Cheese and Apple Casserole

The recipe is so simple and the ingredients so ordinary that it is easy to underrate this dish – until you eat it! The combination of apple, cheese and cider counteracts the richness of the pork to make an unusual main course. We used belly of pork, as Mary Kingsley does, with the rind removed and boned, but you could use any of the other cheaper cuts of pork.

For 4 people
  1½ lb (720 g) pork, cubed
  ½ lb (240 g/2 cups) onions, sliced
  2 large cooking apples, peeled, cored and sliced
  flour, salt, pepper, nutmeg
  ⅜ pint (2·27 decilitres/just under 1 cup) dry cider
  6 oz (180 g/1½ cups) grated Cheddar cheese

Brown the pork quickly, together with the onion, in a little hot oil or dripping. Put the meat and onion in a casserole. Sprinkle flour over juices left in the frying pan, gradually add cider and seasoning, stir until thickened and pour over meat and onion in casserole. Cover with sliced apple and casserole lid and cook for one hour at Gas Mark 4 (350°F/180°C). Then add the grated cheese, increase the oven temperature to Gas Mark 6 (400°F/200°C) and cook uncovered for half an hour.

Steamed Date and Walnut Pudding

This is very good served hot with home-made custard sauce or cold whipped cream. Cold, it tastes like delicious walnut cake.

For 6 people
  4 oz (120 g/½ cup) butter
  4 oz (120 g/¾ cup) caster sugar
  3 standard eggs
  *4 oz (120 g/1 cup) flour (self-raising or plain with a little baking
    powder)*

¼ teaspoon vanilla essence
3 oz (90 g/¾ cup) walnuts
3 oz (90 g/¾ cup) dates, chopped and stoned

Cream the butter and sugar well, beat in the eggs. Fold in the flour, add vanilla essence and fold in nuts and dates. Put into a steamer, or over a saucepan of boiling water and steam for 1½ to 2 hours, checking occasionally that the saucepan has not boiled dry.

Prince Albert's Pudding

This variation, which Queen Victoria's husband was very fond of, is made in the same way, but substituting peel and raisins for the nuts and dates and adding a heaped teaspoonful of mace before cooking.

WEST COUNTRY

Avon, Cornwall, Devon, Somerset, Western Dorset, Wiltshire and the Isles of Scilly

LEUSDON LODGE (B)
Poundsgate, Dartmoor, Devon
Tel: Poundsgate 304
Open 12 noon to 10 pm (last orders 9.30 pm)
Teas, traditional Sunday lunch
Closed Monday

Dartmoor in the sunshine, with the wild ponies roaming free, is a feast for jaded city eyes. But this is Jekyll and Hyde country: on a wet and windy night it turns into a landscape out of Victorian melodrama.

It was just such a wild night when we came to Leusdon Lodge on Easter Sunday. Experience had prepared us for restricted service and most things off the menu. But to our delight, we found a warm and friendly country house, a varied menu and honest food cooked specially for us. We were late, so we had the panelled dining room to ourselves, but extra fires had been turned on and a candle lit on the table. The food was simple and very good – really rare juicy steak, an aromatic venison casserole, floury potatoes, crisp cauliflower and carrots and a delicious home-made pie with an unusual combination of flavours, pear and rhubarb.

The proprietors, Neelia and Denis Hutchins, have been there for 20 years and at first just did bed and breakfast – the large, granite-built house has spectacular views over 20 miles of beautiful Devonshire countryside. Gradually they started to do simple food. Today Mrs Hutchins prides herself on the fact that her guests never have the same dish twice during their stay. She specialises in good old-fashioned home cooking, even baking her own bread and rolls, and makes the most of the very good local produce (cream and cider feature largely in her dishes). She gets a number of overseas visitors and finds this a challenge to show that English food can be really good.

An interesting feature of Leusdon Lodge is the carver meals. A joint of

your choice (ordered in advance) is cooked and served with fresh vegetables. You carve and serve it as you wish and with it comes a plastic bag
so you take home the left-overs. The cost of the joint is the same whether
there are two or eight at the table – there is a small additional charge per
person to cover the vegetables and service.

Another speciality is the Christmas fare (ten courses for lunch and
people stayed on for tea!); as space is limited you are advised to book
early.

We had our coffee in the lounge, a comfortable family room with a
blazing fire, a friendly dog and deep sofas on which you can curl up with
your shoes off. We made a mental note to come back and stay to explore
the wonderful moorland and countryside from a place that really is a
home from home.

RECIPES FROM LEUSDON LODGE

Venison Casserole

For 6–8 people
2–3 lb (960 g/1·440 kg) stewing venison
1 bottle brown ale or Guinness
1 large sliced onion
a few juniper berries, crushed
crushed black peppercorns
dripping or oil and butter for browning

Cut the meat into cubes and marinate it in the ale with the sliced onion,
the crushed peppercorns and juniper berries for 24 hours. Then drain
the meat (keep the marinade), brown it in a little dripping (or butter
and oil mixed) add the marinade and cook it for about an hour, or until
meat is tender, at Gas Mark 3 (325°F/160°C). Check the seasoning and
serve with mashed potatoes and crisp green cabbage.

Pear and Rhubarb Pie

For 6 people
1 lb (480 g) rhubarb
1½ lb (720 g) pears
3 oz (90 g/⅓ cup) sugar

The pastry:

    8 oz (240 g/2 cups) self-raising flour
    3 oz (90 g/6 tablespoons) lard
    2 oz (60 g/4 tablespoons) margarine
    water to mix

Cook the peeled pears and rhubarb with the sugar (you may need a little water; we didn't add any). Make the pastry by rubbing the fats into the flour and mixing with water. Roll it out and fill a 10-inch flan ring, put in the rhubarb and pear filling and cook at Gas Mark 7 (425°F/220°C) for about 20 minutes. It's good hot or cold, with double cream.

VILLA MAGDALA

Henrietta Road, Bath, Avon
Tel: Bath 25836
Open for bed and breakfasts (7.45 pm to 9 am) between Easter
and October inclusive

'If you want to eat well in England,' said the late Somerset Maugham, 'you must eat three breakfasts a day.' We agree with him that the traditional English breakfast is better than any other variety, and are happy to report that you can still enjoy a good old-fashioned spread in a number of places. Villa Magdala is one of them. Sally and George Fuller, the owners, offer an excellent personal service. Breakfast – aptly described on the guest-house literature as 'full' – is cooked by George. Starters include fresh and stewed fruits, juices and cereals, then there is generally a choice of eggs cooked in five different ways, local bacon, sausages or ham

(George buys a whole green Wiltshire fore-end, cuts joints from it to simmer slowly in stock); Scotch Finnan Haddock, or Shetland Kippers. But the menu varies according to the season, and you might find such delights as potted meat, or brawn (see recipe below).

Villa Magdala – a large, comfortable house built in the last century – is five minutes' walk from the centre of Bath, and ideally placed for sightseeing in this beautiful city. All rooms have baths or showers and private toilets.

RECIPE FROM VILLA MAGDALA

Brawn

1 pig's head quartered, but leaving the tongue whole
¼ pint (1·5 decilitres/⅔ cup) wine vinegar
¼ pint (1·5 decilitres/⅔ cup) sweet white wine

Tied up in a muslin bag:
½ lemon
sprig each of parsley, sage and thyme
½ teaspoonful of mace
6 cloves
1 clove of garlic
1 onion roughly chopped
4 bay leaves
salt and freshly ground black pepper to taste

Put the washed and cleaned quartered head and the whole tongue into a large saucepan with the bag of flavourings, the vinegar and wine and add only sufficient water to cover. Bring to the boil, then reduce heat to a very slow simmer for 3–4 hours, when the meat should come easily off the bone. Take off heat, remove head and tongue and as soon as they are cool enough to handle, strip meat from bones and ears and skin the tongue. Discard any coarse skin. Leave tongue whole but chop rest of meat into sugar-cube-sized pieces. Remove muslin bag and strain liquid. Skim off any fat and reduce to about ⅓. Return the meat (not the tongue) to the reduced liquor and bring to the boil again. Immediately remove from heat. Put about 1-inch (25mm) depth of meat in a suitably sized container. Place tongue in centre and put rest of meat around and over it. Add enough of any remaining liquor to cover. Place a weight on top and leave to set solid in a cool place for 24 hours. Dip the container in hot water to free the brawn and then turn out.

LANHYDROCK HOUSE (A)

Lanhydrock, Bodmin, Cornwall
Tel: Bodmin 3320
Open 11 am to 6 pm (last orders lunch 2 pm, tea 5.30 pm)
April 1 to October 31

Glorious grounds, a beautiful house, exquisite furniture – you're in one of England's many stately homes. A sign indicates Refreshments and all too often you plunge from Tudor splendour or 18th-century elegance into 20th-century squalor – the cafeteria with stacking chairs, sandwiches in invincible cellophane, tea in paper cups, iced lollies and orange drinks.

Lanhydrock House is a shining exception to this dreary rule; it provides freshly-cooked food well served in a charming restaurant.

The house is set in beautiful grounds in the valley of the River Fowey, between Liskeard and Lostwithiel. There are beech woods, tall banks of rhododendrons and camellias flowering against the grey stone walls of the house. Once the site of an Augustinian priory, the estate belonged to one family, the Robartes, from 1620 to 1969, and was given to the National Trust in 1953. Only the pretty gatehouse, the porch and the North wing are left of the original 17th-century house, gutted by fire in 1881. The rebuilt house is interesting for the vivid picture it gives of life in a wealthy Victorian household.

There is a choice of two restaurants – one serves light refreshments, the other a three-course lunch and tea with home-made cakes. The menu changes daily and offers home-made soups, a buffet of unusual salads, cold flans, luscious home-baked ham and two or three hot dishes including Cornish specialities like Leek Pie. They bake their own bread and we drank local draught cider, strong and very good. The restaurant is pretty with a cheerful log fire and fresh flowers on every table and prices are a very pleasant surprise.

Other National Trust properties in Devon and Cornwall which specialise in good home cooking at competitive prices are:

172

Arlington Court,
Shirwell, Near Barnstaple, Devon
Georgian property in very large estate

Castle Drogo,
Drewsteignton, Exeter, Devon
Unusual 20th-century castle

Cotehele House,
St Dominic, Saltash, Devon
Tudor house, restaurant in barn

Killerton House,
Broadclyst, Exeter, Devon
Country mansion set in lovely gardens

Knightshayes Court,
Tiverton, Devon
Victorian mansion in beautiful gardens

Saltram House,
Plympton, Plymouth, Devon
Restaurant in lovely Tudor kitchen inside Georgian Mansion

Trerice Manor,
Kestle Mill, Newquay, Cornwall
Restaurant in Cornish barn attached to Manor

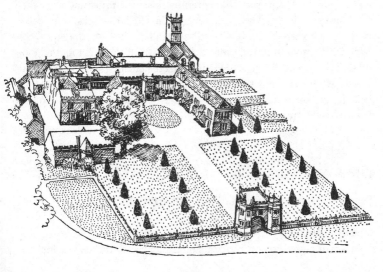

RECIPE FROM LANHYDROCK HOUSE

Likkypie

Or Leek Pie, is a Cornish speciality which used to be served on high days and holidays. You can make it without the pastry crust, when it comes out rather like a leek soufflé.

For 4 people
    10–12 leeks
    ¼ lb (240 g) sliced unsmoked bacon
    ¼ pint (1·5 decilitres/⅔ cup) double cream
    2 eggs (separated)
    ¼ pint (1·5 decilitres/⅔ cup) milk
    salt and pepper

The pastry:
    8 oz (240 g/2 cups) self-raising flour
    2 oz (60 g/4 tablespoons) lard
    2 oz (60 g/4 tablespoons) margarine
    water to mix
    pinch of salt

Clean and chop the leeks, cook them in the milk with salt and pepper for about 5 minutes. Lift them out carefully (keep the milk) and layer them with the bacon in a pie dish. Add the milk in which the leeks were cooked, cover with a pastry lid and bake for half an hour at Gas Mark 4 (350°F/180°C). Remove from the oven, carefully lift off the crust and take out most of the liquid. Beat the egg yolks with the cream, then add the stiffly-beaten whites and put this mixture on the pie, put back the crust and bake in the oven for another 10 minutes. If the pastry is getting too brown, cover it with foil.

THE SAVERNAKE FOREST HOTEL (B)

Savernake, Burbage, near Marlborough, Wiltshire
Tel: Burbage 810206
Open 12 noon to 2 pm (buffet); 7.30 to 9 pm (restaurant)
Restaurant closed to non-residents on Sunday and Monday nights

This pleasant, family-run hotel near the Savernake Forest, with fishing rights along a mile of the nearby Kennet and Avon canal offers good food at reasonable prices in peaceful surroundings.

A feature of the hotel is the popular wine and buffet bar, open every day of the week for lunch with salads, pâtés, fresh-cut sandwiches and a range of hot dishes to accompany the choice of over 50 wines – including old English country wines.

Dinner, served in the pleasant restaurant, is more elaborate with a wide choice of unusual English dishes like the gooseberry and wine sauce which gives chicken a delicate flavour. A friendly welcome and careful service reflect the family's maxim – 'We like to treat our customers as we would like to be treated ourselves.'

RECIPE FROM THE SAVERNAKE FOREST HOTEL

Gooseberry Chicken

For 4–6 people

   a 3½–4 lb (1·680–1·920 kg) chicken, skinned and jointed
   1 teaspoon powdered ginger
   1 pint (0·57 litres/2⅔ cups) cooked gooseberries
   1 glass gooseberry wine (or white wine)
   1–2 tablespoons brown sugar
   1 pint (0·57 litres/2⅔ cups) white sauce made with half milk and
     half single cream
   salt and pepper

Season the chicken joints with salt and pepper and place in a fireproof casserole. Make the white sauce with butter and flour and ½ pint (0·28 litres/1⅓ cups) each of milk and single cream. If you are using fresh gooseberries cook them in the wine with the ginger and as much of the brown sugar as you want – they should taste sharp but not sour. If you are using tinned gooseberries, drain them and heat in the wine with the ginger. Combine gooseberries with the white sauce, check for salt and pepper and pour over the chicken. Cover the casserole and cook in the oven at Gas Mark 3 (325°F/160°C) until chicken is tender.

KING HARRY HOTEL (A, B)

King Harry Ferry, Feock, Truro, Cornwall
Tel: Devoran 862202
Open 12 noon to 2 pm (last orders 1.45); 7 pm to 8.30 pm (last orders 7.45)
Closed to non-residents November to January

You approach the King Harry Hotel in the most romantic way. From Roseland, the car ferry sails slowly across King Harry's Passage where three rivers – the Truro, Tresilian and the Fal – join to flow between beautiful banks towards the sea. From Truro, you drive along a climbing wooded road, here and there looking down on winding creeks.

The hotel was once the farm of the Trelissick estate (now a National Trust property with gardens open to the public). Outside it is all mellow stone, intimate paved courtyards, banks of hydrangeas and rhododendrons and mature trees. Inside it is a delightful mixture of well-designed modern furniture and carefully chosen antiques, reflecting the taste of its owners, Ted Kirkham and his Swedish born wife Margaretha.

For years they toured the world as Ted edited a leading tourism magazine. Now they have settled in this beautiful and peaceful corner of Cornwall; staying there is like sharing their home, for there is nothing impersonal about this small and immaculate hotel. All around are signs of the trouble taken to make guests comfortable and welcome. We arrived for dinner on Easter Saturday to find chocolate eggs by our plate and an Easter tree hung with eggs and coloured feathers in the centre of the dining room – an old Swedish custom symbolising the arrival of Spring. The view from the dining room is breathtaking, beautiful parkland sweeping down to the water of the estuary. The food is simple, wholesome and well-cooked – the coffee set out on a handsome old pine table for guests to help themselves.

There is no set lunch but snacks are prepared to order at the bar – a Ferryman's lunch consisting of prawns and the local smoked mackerel, freshly made quiches and a touch of Sweden – a mini smorgasbord which includes ham, beef, sardines, egg, pâté, cheese and coleslaw.

There are facilities for boating, fishing, riding, tennis and golf; lovely walks all round the hotel and small creeks and a secluded beach to explore – an idyllic place to get away from it all.

Beef Olives in Red Wine Sauce

For 6–8 people

6–8 rump or sirloin steaks, lightly beaten and trimmed

(We used thinly-cut top rump, gently beaten out by the butcher. It's cheaper, just takes a little longer to cook.)

The filling:

1 large chopped onion
½ green pepper, de-seeded and chopped
3 oz (90 g) sliced mushrooms
2–3 rashers streaky bacon
1–2 eggs
4 oz (120 g) veal forcemeat (made by mincing 4 oz pie veal
*   through a coarse blade twice, and through a fine blade twice,*
*   till it resembles sausage meat)*
white breadcrumbs
1 clove garlic
a little Worcester Sauce
salt and freshly ground black pepper
4 tablespoons cooking oil

The wine sauce:

½ pint (0·28 litres/1⅓ cups) brown sauce – see recipe under Tripe
*   and Onions, Drake's Restaurant, London section) or you can*
*   cheat and use a stock cube and if necessary thicken the sauce*
*   with small knobs of butter rolled in flour*
½–¾ pint (0·28–0·42 litres/1⅓–2 cups) red wine
1 large sliced onion
½ green pepper, de-seeded and chopped
3–5 oz (90–150 g) mushrooms, sliced
1 dessertspoon tomato purée
1 clove garlic
3 oz (90 g/6 tablespoons) butter
3–4 oz (90–120 g/¾–1 cup) flour
4 tablespoons cooking oil

To make the filling, heat the oil gently in a pan, fry the onion and pepper till softened but not coloured. Add the chopped bacon and the veal forcemeat; let them brown, then add the garlic and sliced mushrooms and fry for a few minutes. Add enough breadcrumbs to give the consistency of a crumble. Remove from heat and season with a dash of Worcester Sauce, salt and pepper. When it's cooled add enough beaten egg to bind the mixture.

Now lay the steaks out on a board, spoon a little of the mixture onto the middle of each, roll up and tie securely. Heat the oil in a pan and brown the olives all over to seal. Remove to an earthenware dish. Lightly fry the onions, peppers, mushrooms and garlic. Place this mixture on top of olives in the dish. Melt the butter in the pan, stir in the tomato purée and flour, slowly add the stock or brown sauce and wine alternately until the sauce resembles a thickened gravy. If you like, add herbs of your choice; if sauce is not thick enough add a few knobs of butter rolled in flour. Season and pour over olives. Cook in a moderate oven, Gas Mark 4 (350°F/180°C) for 1–1½ hours or until the meat feels tender. Remove strings and serve hot with mashed potatoes and a green vegetable.

GEORGE AND PILGRIMS HOTEL AND RESTAURANT (B)

1 High Street, Glastonbury, Somerset
Tel: Glastonbury 31146
Open 12.30 pm to 2 pm; 7 pm to 9.30 pm
Closed Sunday evening but bar snacks available

Glastonbury Abbey was built near the site of the first Christian church in Britain, and pilgrims still come to worship here on the last Saturday in June each year. The twelfth- and thirteenth-century ruins of the Abbey with King Arthur and Queen Guinevere's tomb, the remains of the first daub and wattle church, and the flowering Holy Thorn tree where Joseph of Arimathea is said to have planted his staff, are open to visitors – who can also enjoy the hospitality of the George and Pilgrims, just as others before them have done for over five hundred years.

John de Selwood, Abbot of Glastonbury, rebuilt this Inn in 1475 'for the accommodation of the ever-increasing number of pilgrims, palmers and notaries to the Abbey', and the stone façade with ecclesiastical overtones has not altered much since. Inside, stone flags, ancient beams, mullioned windows – even four-poster beds in some of the bedrooms –

preserve the medieval character of the inn while twentieth-century amenities make it very comfortable for guests. If you are attracted by ghosts, there is a haunted bedroom known as 'the Monk's Cell' while historians may prefer to sleep in the room where Henry VIII watched the burning of the Abbey in 1539.

The hotel specialises in traditional English food (pigeons for your pigeon pie have probably been shot by the owner, Major Jack Richardson) and *real* English Ale.

RECIPES FROM GEORGE AND PILGRIMS

Summer Fish Salad

For 4–6 people
1 lb (480 g) any white fish, cooked
½ lb (240 g) prawns, peeled
½ cucumber
sprigs of fresh mint
the juice of 1 lemon
vinaigrette dressing
freshly milled black pepper
white wine to taste
watercress and a few black grapes for garnish

Flake the fish and remove any skin and bones, chill it with the prawns. Peel the cucumber and chop into cubes. Strip the mint, reserving some leaves for decoration. Combine the flaked fish, prawns, cucumber and mint leaves. Carefully toss this mixture in the combined vinaigrette, lemon juice, wine and pepper. Serve on a bed of watercress, garnished with lemon twists and halved grapes.

Simple Simon's Fillet of Pork

For 4 people
2 pork fillets
4 oz (120 g/½ cup) butter
8 oz (240 g) mushrooms
2 tablespoons Gordon's English Vineyard mustard
¼ pint (1·5 decilitres/⅔ cup) single cream
salt

Trim the fillets of all fat and sinew, cut in half and flatten each half. Coat one side of each fillet with the mustard. Melt the butter in a large frying pan and when the foam subsides, add the sliced mushrooms. Cook for a minute then add the fillets, mustard side down. Cook for 3–4 minutes on each side. Lift out fillets and keep warm on a serving plate. Return the pan to the heat and add the cream, stirring all the time until the sauce boils and thickens, check seasoning. Pour over fillets and serve at once.

Pigeon Pie

For 4 people
  2 pigeons
  1 onion, roughly chopped
  4 oz (120 g) sliced mushrooms
  2 carrots, sliced
  ½ pint (0·28 litres/1¼ cups) red wine
  2 oz (60 g/½ cup) flour
  1 tablespoon tomato purée
  ¾ lb (360 g) puff pastry (frozen)
  1 egg
  salt and freshly milled black pepper

Cut the cleaned pigeons in half and trim off the wings and claws. Place the trimmings in a pan and cover with 1½ pints (0·85 litres/4 cups) of water and red wine mixed. Bring to the boil and simmer for 1½ hours. Place the pigeon halves, the onion, carrots and mushrooms in a casserole dish and mix in the flour and tomato purée. Pour over the stock and braise in the oven at Gas Mark 3 (325°F/160°C) for about 2 hours. After 2 hours place the pigeons and enough of the sauce to come half way up the pigeons in a pie dish and cover with the puff pastry. Brush with the beaten egg and bake in the oven until the pastry is well risen and brown, about 20–30 minutes at Gas Mark 6 (400°F/200°C).

THE SEAFOOD RESTAURANT (B)

Station Road, Padstow, Cornwall
Tel: Padstow 532485
Open 12 noon to 2 pm; 7 to 10 pm
Closed on Mondays, and from November to mid-March

Padstow is a fine, sheltered harbour on the north coast of Cornwall. Little yachts swing at anchor side by side with sturdy fishing boats, and piles of lobster pots stacked on the quay bear silent witness to the main business of the town.

Further up this coast is Polzeath, with its gentle sweep of sandy beach; the old lobster port and former haven for smugglers, Port Isaac, making a deep gash in the rugged coastline; Tintagel, where the ruins of King Arthur's mystical castle overhang the sea; and Boscastle – an enchanting fishing village where you can climb a steep cliff path to watch the waves far below battering on the perilous rocky entrance.

Local fish is a feature of almost all the hotels and restaurants in the area, but it is the speciality of Rick Stein's quayside restaurant in Padstow. Here, in what used to be a granary and has been converted downstairs to a pleasant whitewashed restaurant hung with fishing nets, you can eat crab, sole, lobster, salmon, cray-fish and other sea foods so freshly caught that you can still taste the sea in them! Simple cooking and home-made sauces bring out the fine flavour of the fish, which is served with salads or lightly cooked vegetables. There is meat on the menu, and home-made puddings served with clotted cream for those who have got room.

RECIPE FROM THE SEAFOOD RESTAURANT

Seafood Thermidor

For 4–5 people
  1 lb (480 g) cooked seafood

The Seafood Restaurant use 4 oz (120 g) each of lobster, crab meat, prawns or shrimps and scallops, but you can work out your own variations.

4 oz (120 g) fresh button mushrooms
2½ oz (75 g/5 tablespoons) butter
2 oz (60 g/½ cup) flour
1 pint (0·57 litres/2⅔ cups) milk
1 pint (0·57 litres/2⅔ cups) fish stock
2 egg yolks
a little lemon juice
4 oz (120 g/1 cup) grated Cheddar cheese for sauce

mustard to taste
½ pint (0·28 litres/1¼ cups) white wine
1 small finely chopped onion
chopped tarragon, parsley
salt and freshly ground pepper
4 oz (120 g/1 cup) grated cheese (¾ Cheddar, ¼ Parmesan)
   for topping
pinch of paprika

Heat the milk and fish stock, melt 2 oz (60 g/4 tablespoons) of the butter in a pan, add the flour and cook gently for 2 minutes. Gradually add the milk and stock, stirring constantly until sauce is smooth and leave to simmer for 20 minutes, stirring occasionally. Meanwhile, cut the mushrooms into thin slices and blanch them in water with a little butter, lemon juice and salt. Strain and add them to the mixed seafood. Sweat the chopped onion in ½ oz left-over butter, then add the wine, parsley, tarragon and pepper. Let it reduce by two thirds and add to the sauce. Then add the grated cheese and as much mustard as you like – it should not be sharp – use English mustard powder mixed with a little lemon juice. Finally mix a little of the sauce with the two egg yolks, whisk well and blend into the sauce. DO NOT LET IT BOIL AGAIN. The sauce should be the consistency of mayonnaise; if it's too thin, simmer very gently; if too thick, add a little milk. Spoon half the sauce into a shallow ovenproof dish, place the mushrooms and seafood on top, coat with the remainder of the sauce, place in a warm oven long enough merely to heat up the seafood. Then sprinkle the top with the grated Cheddar and Parmesan cheese and a pinch of paprika and place under the grill until golden brown. Serve with parsley and lemon quarters.

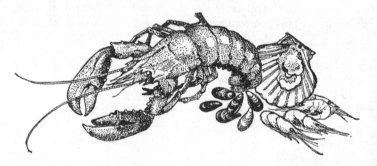

TALLAND BAY HOTEL (B)

Talland-by-Looe, Cornwall
Tel: Polperro 228
Open 7 am to 9 pm daily; traditional Sunday lunch
Closed December and January

'Do not come if you seek promenades, piers, cinemas, discothèques, hustle, bustle and noise . . . ' says the Talland Bay Hotel brochure, and when you get there you see at once why. Talland Bay is gloriously unspoilt; miles of uninterrupted green countryside running down to sandy and rocky beaches, protected by encircling cliffs. A tiny lane climbs abruptly from the Bay, up past the hotel, which is a long, low building dating back to the 16th century. Inside, large rooms comfortably furnished with antiques, deep sofas and armchairs, welcome hotel guests during ten months of the year.

The hotel faces south, 150 feet above sea level, overlooking two dramatic headlands and blue-green seas as far as the Eddystone lighthouse, 15 miles away. There are 2½ acres of garden, with sub-tropical plants as well as English country flowers, and from here you can walk across the cliffs to Looe on one side, or to Polperro on the other. The L-shape of the building encloses a heated outdoor swimming pool, round which guests can eat light lunches in summer.

Dinner is served in a panelled dining room, with white cloths, shining silver, fresh flowers and candles. The food is good, plain cooking, using local produce often including vegetables from the hotel garden. The choice is sensibly narrowed to two or three really good dishes for each course of the table d'hôte, and an excellent sweet trolley.

Major and Mrs Mayman, the owners, run the hotel with imagination and care to make guests feel as relaxed as if they were at home. Service is attentive yet unobtrusive. There is plenty to do and see locally, and – out of season – you can come here for a week's landscape painting or bird-watching under expert guidance.

RECIPES FROM TALLAND BAY HOTEL

Ginger Ice Cream

For 4–6 people
 4 large eggs

5 oz (150 g/¾ cup) icing sugar
a little vanilla flavouring
½ pint (0·28 litres/1¼ cups) double cream
½ pint (0·28 litres/1¼ cups) single cream
chopped stem ginger

Beat the eggs and sugar till thick, whip the cream together (not too thick) and fold into egg mixture, add the chopped ginger and freeze.

Crab Au Gratin

Make this in individual ovenproof ramekins. Use frozen crab if fresh is not available. Give each person enough brown and white meat to half fill the ramekins. Warm the crab through, then pack down, add a touch of brandy, a little double cream, cover with grated Parmesan cheese and pop under a hot grill till it bubbles. Serve at once.

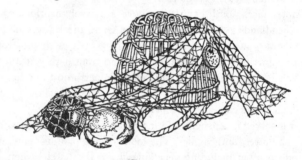

HOME FARM HOTEL (B)

Wilmington, Nr Honiton, Devon
Tel: Wilmington 278
Open 12.30 to 1.45 pm; 7.30 to 9 pm
Closed Sunday night

As the name suggests, Home Farm Hotel started out as a farm. The outside, with traditional thatched roof and rough-cast white walls, probably looks much the same as when it was built, in the 16th century. Inside, too, still has the feeling of a farm, with dark oak furniture, chintz curtains, and gleaming copper and brass, but with the advantage of 20th-century luxuries such as central heating and private bathrooms for several of the bedrooms.

The present owners, Myles and Monique Craston, moved in 1975 and, under their expert management, the hotel has acquired a very good reputation for comfort and food. 'We always recommend our guests to have the table d'hôte menu, which we change at every meal,' says Myles Craston.

The day we lunched, the table d'hôte, with dishes like Savoury Chicken Pancakes or Fillets of Lemon Sole; home-made terrine or vegetable soup; and a choice of sweets or Stilton cheese, was wonderful value and very well cooked.

Our vegetables were from the garden – new potatoes and cauliflower in a white sauce. 'When we came, the vegetable garden of about an acre presented quite a problem,' Myles Craston told us. 'But we advertised for someone who might like to take it off our hands, and now we buy about as much from our "tenant" as he can grow. Things like leeks are washed in the stream running through the grounds and brought to the kitchen door, where we weigh them and pay on the spot.'

The kitchen is under the supervision of a surprisingly young chef,

Sue, who is Cordon Bleu trained, and a number of the regular dishes on the hotel menu are made from her recipes.

Before coming to Home Farm Hotel, Myles Craston was head of one of the biggest hotel chains in Canada and his professional expertise shows. Every comfort, every amenity and service is provided for guests, even to an Ordnance Survey map pinpointing 14 things to do or see locally hung in one of the reception rooms.

RECIPES FROM HOME FARM HOTEL

Baked Gammon with Cumberland Sauce

> 4 or 5 lb piece (1·920 kg to 2·400 kg) of green (unsmoked)
>   gammon
> 1 large onion
> 2 large carrots
> 1 bay leaf
> black peppercorns
> Demerara sugar to coat
> cloves to decorate

Soak the gammon overnight. Next day, place the gammon in a large pan, cover it with fresh water, add the chopped onion and carrots, the bay leaf and peppercorns. Boil it for about 2 hours (a little less for a 4 lb piece) on a low heat on top of the stove, or until the rind comes away easily from the fat. Remove gammon from the water and let it cool. Strip off the rind, score the fat and gently sprinkle the fat with Demerara sugar. Put in a roasting pan in a fairly hot oven, Gas Mark 5 (375°F/190°C), until the sugar has caramelised. Remove from roasting pan, decorate with cloves and serve hot with hot Cumberland sauce.

Cumberland Sauce

> 2 oranges
> 2 tablespoons redcurrant jelly
> 2 measures of port (about ¼ pint/1·5 decilitres/⅔ cup)
> 1 teaspoon French mustard
> salt and pepper
> a little arrowroot if needed

Peel the rind from both oranges and cut it into thin strips. Squeeze the juice from the oranges and put it into a small saucepan with the port; bring to the boil then add the strips of rind, the redcurrant jelly and the mustard. Heat slowly until the jelly has dissolved and the sauce has reached a coating consistency. If you are adding the arrowroot, do so while the sauce is at boiling temperature and stir all the time. Serve very hot.

HOLBROOK HOUSE HOTEL (B)

Castle Cary Road, Wincanton, Somerset
Tel: Wincanton 32377
Open 8.15 am to 9.15 am; 12.45 to 1.30 pm; 7.30 to 8.30 pm

One of the glories of England is an abundance of fine old country houses, often spacious and set in acres of lovely grounds. One such is Holbrook House Hotel, two miles west of Wincanton. The first record of a house on this site goes back to 1327; this was completely rebuilt in the sixteenth century, and then again considerably enlarged in 1846. It became an hotel under the present owners in 1945, with large, comfortable rooms (warm in winter, cool in summer); friendly service and good English food. In the grounds, there is a heated swimming pool, squash and tennis courts, croquet lawn, and a walled vegetable garden that supplies your table. The restaurant specialises in using local meats, and fresh fish from the coast. Cornish smoked mackerel and pilchard are delivered weekly by train, and fresh Dabs and Lemon Soles when possible. During the winter months, there's always pheasant and hare on the menu. You can sample a number of 'Taste of England' dishes here, including the two that we give recipes for below – Local veal cooked with Cheddar cheese, and Chicken Wessex style with a honey and Cerne Abbas mead sauce.

RECIPES FROM HOLBROOK HOUSE HOTEL

Chicken Wessex, with a honey and 'Cerne Abbas' mead sauce

For 2 people
   Allow one 2 lb (960 g) fresh chicken

5 oz (150 g/10 tablespoons) butter
5 oz (150 g/10 tablespoons) lard
seasoned flour
1 lemon
5 oz (150 g/⅔ cup) honey
3 oz (90 g/½ cup) brown sugar
¼ pint (1·5 decilitres/⅔ cup) mead
1 cooking apple
1 bunch watercress (for garnish)
1 teaspoon nutmeg
1 teaspoon cinnamon
½ pint (0·28 litres/1¼ cups) brown sauce (see under Drakes, in London
    section, in recipe for Tripe and Onions)

Clean and draw the chicken; cut in half and remove backbone. Roll in seasoned flour. Melt half the butter with half the lard in a frying pan; cook chicken halves in the fat for about 20 minutes, turning regularly, until they are golden brown.

Mead Sauce

Melt the remaining butter and lard in a saucepan; peel and finely slice the apple and cook slowly in melted fats; add brown sugar and lemon juice, stirring; pour in honey and mead and let simmer for a few minutes; add nutmeg and cinnamon. Pour in the brown sauce, simmer for 5 minutes, strain over the chicken halves and garnish with watercress to serve.

Veal with Cheddar Cheese and Fresh Herbs

For 4 people
    2 lb (960 g) fresh leg of veal
    4 oz (120 g) mixed chopped herbs – parsley, thyme, sage, lemon
        thyme, chives and a bay leaf
    8 oz (240 g/2 cups) Cheddar cheese, grated
    2 pints (1·14 litres/5¼ cups) white sauce
    seasoned flour
    4 oz (120 g/8 tablespoons) butter
    ½ pint (0·28 litres/1¼ cups) dry cider, or stock
    1 lettuce

Slice veal thinly and roll in seasoned flour. Melt butter in pan and cook veal for 5 minutes, turning often, until golden brown. Add cider or stock and simmer for a further 5 minutes before adding the herbs and half the cheese. Mix in the white sauce and bring to the boil. Arrange the veal on a fire-proof plate and pour over the sauce; sprinkle on the remainder of the cheese and melt under the grill. Decorate with the lettuce.

WOOLVERTON HOUSE HOTEL (C)

Woolverton, Bath, BA3 6QS
Tel: Beckington 415
Restaurant open 7 pm to 10 pm (Monday to Saturday)
Closed Sunday evening (not the hotel)

Before opening Woolverton House as a 'restaurant with rooms' in January, 1978, the owners – Peter and Jennifer Conway – had already run a most successful restaurant in Wiltshire. So they brought with them invaluable knowledge as well as a stock of good wines! Jennifer changes the menu for the restaurant every four to six weeks; there's always a selection of interesting starters (home-made soup, terrine, hors d'oeuvres or fish appetisers); half a dozen or so main courses including at least one English dish like 'Somerset Pork', cooked with apricots, cream, cider and rosemary; and a wide selection of puddings from the trolley which taste as good as they look.

Though the Conways have made their reputation on their good food, rooms in this sturdy, early Victorian house are fully modernised with their own bathrooms and colour televisions. Woolverton – less than 15 minutes from Bath – is an excellent place for sight-seeing locally, or for breaking a long journey to the west coast.

RECIPES FROM WOOLVERTON HOUSE HOTEL

Prawns Charles (named after the owners' son!)

For 4 people
2 small cucumbers
4 oz (120 g) mushrooms
2 oz (60 g/4 tablespoons) butter
3–4 oz (90–120 g) shelled prawns
1 teaspoon flour

⅛ pint (0·07 litres/⅓ cup) chicken stock
⅛ pint (0·07 litres/⅓ cup) single cream
salt and pepper
herbs for garnish – chives, basil or dill

Chop the fresh, washed cucumbers – without peeling – into large cubes. Blanch for ¾ minute in boiling, salted water; drain. Melt butter in pan and add sliced mushrooms; cook for a few minutes, shaking all the time. Add cucumber and simmer (covered) on low heat for 2 or 3 minutes. Blend in flour. Stir in stock and cream. Bring slowly to the boil and season to taste. Simmer for a further 2 or 3 minutes and finally stir in chopped prawns and heat through. Garnish with herbs before serving – you can serve with croutons, if you like.

Roast Rack of Lamb with Tomatoes and Onions

For 4–6 people
  2 racks of lamb
  ½ lb (240 g) onions
  1 lb (480 g) tomatoes
  ¼ bottle white wine
  ½ pint (0·28 litres/1⅓ cups) stock
  4 oz (120 g/1 cup) grated cheese mixed with 4 oz (120 g/2 cups)
    breadcrumbs
  oil

Roughly chop onions and fry in oil till lightly browned. Skin and roughly chop tomatoes, place these and fried onions in baking dish. Trim excess fat from lamb; brush with oil and coat with cheese and breadcrumbs. Place on top of tomatoes and onions. Pour in stock and wine. Roast in oven at Gas Mark 6 (400°F/200°C) for about 1 to 1½ hours, depending on how pink you like the lamb to be.

Redcurrant and Almond Roulade

For 4–6 people
  6 eggs
  4 oz (120 g/¾ cup) ground almonds
  8 oz (240 g/just under 1¼ cups) caster sugar
  1 oz (30 g/¼ cup) plain flour
  6 oz (180 g) redcurrants

almond essence (to taste)
½ pint (0·28 litres/1⅓ cups) whipping cream

Separate eggs. Beat whites till firm. Beat yolks with sugar until light and creamy. Add almond essence to taste. Add sifted flour and ground almonds to the egg-yolk mixture and fold in the egg whites. Line a swiss-roll tin with greaseproof paper. Add mixture and cook at Gas Mark 4 (350°F/180°C) until golden brown. Turn out and cool. Spread with lightly whipped cream. Sprinkle with redcurrants (saving some for decoration) and roll carefully. Decorate and dust with icing sugar.

Frozen Almond Creams

For 5–6 people
½ pint (0·28 litres/1⅓ cups) double cream
2 oz (60 g/⅓ cup) caster sugar
2 egg whites
4 oz (120 g/¾ cup) chopped, toasted almonds
salt
Sherry, Marsala, Madeira or any Cognac (Woolverton House vary this addition regularly)

Beat egg whites; add sugar and salt and continue beating till mixture is visibly stiff with a shiny look. Whip cream and fold into egg mixture with most of the almonds, but saving two spoons of these for decorating later. Stir in the chosen alcohol, to taste, and spoon into individual soufflé dishes. Freeze for 4 hours. Decorate with the rest of the almonds.

SOUTH OF ENGLAND

Hampshire, Eastern Dorset and the Isle of Wight

THE HEN AND CHICKEN INN (B)

Froyle, Alton, Hampshire
Tel: Bentley 2115
Open 12 noon to 2 pm; 7 pm to 10 pm

'Four hundred years of good cheer and hospitality' could well be the Hen and Chicken's slogan. Standing on the main road from Winchester to Canterbury, one of the oldest important highways in the country, it has numbered among its patrons over the ages highwaymen, pilgrims, merchants on the way to the great fairs at Winchester and Guildford and local farmers.

For many years the Bishops of Winchester employed five mounted men-at-arms to protect travellers along the road during the period of the great St Giles Fair. Signs of a quick getaway for highwaymen are still visible in the inn; a steep staircase leads from the kitchen to a trap door in the floor of an upstairs room, and there are signs of exits to both the cellar and the chimney.

The inn has a Georgian façade built in 1760 after a raging fire destroyed the upper storeys of the house, but the interior has preserved its sixteenth-century architecture. The inn specialises in traditional English food and many of the dishes are based on very old recipes, like the Hare in Ale and Saffron for which we pass on the recipe, which can be traced back to 1378. The delicious dessert made from cream, cottage cheese, honey and egg yolks is sixteenth century, like the house, and the Eggs with Anchovies date back to 1695. You can choose from a three- or four-course Old English dinner which changes every few weeks, or from a comprehensive à la carte, or have a light snack in the Buttery.

Eggs with Anchovies

For 4 people
  8 eggs (preferably free range)
  4 shelled walnuts
  12 shelled hazelnuts
  8 anchovy fillets
  ¼ glass dry white wine
  4 slices white bread
  1 oz (30 g/2 tablespoons) butter
  salt and freshly-ground black pepper

Lightly beat the eggs, combine with the white wine. Crush or grind the nuts. Melt the butter in a saucepan, add the eggs and the wine and stir over a low heat until of a slightly soft texture, then mix in the nuts; season. Have ready four slices of buttered toast with the crusts removed, pour the mixture over the toast and arrange two fillets of anchovies on the top of each.

Hare in Ale with Saffron

For 5–6 people
  1 large hare
  1 lb (480 g) onions
  2 oz (60 g/about 1 cup) fresh breadcrumbs
  ¼ teaspoon saffron
  1½ pints (0·85 litres/4 cups) real ale
  salt and freshly ground pepper
  a little dripping or oil and butter for browning

Skin and clean the hare or get your butcher to do so! Cut into segments – approximately 12 pieces. Lightly brown the pieces of hare in a little dripping, or a mixture of oil and butter, in a deep casserole. Then cover the hare with the real ale, add the finely chopped onion and bring to the boil on top of the stove. Put the casserole in the oven and cook at Gas Mark 7 (425°F/220°C) for about 3 hours. Remove from the oven and stir in the breadcrumbs and the saffron. Check seasonings. Continue cooking in the oven until hare is tender and serve with the reduced cooking liquid.

Mon Ami

A French name for what is actually an old English recipe!

For 4–5 people
1 pint (0·57 litres/2⅔ cups) double cream
4 oz (120 g) cottage cheese
2 oz (60 g/about ¼ cup) caster sugar
6 dessertspoons honey
1½ oz (45 g/3 tablespoons) melted butter
4 egg yolks

Carefully boil the cream in a saucepan and allow to cool. Beat the cheese and the caster sugar together and add the honey a little at a time. Lightly fold in the cream, the melted butter and the egg yolks. Pour into a saucepan and cook over a low heat, stirring all the time until the mixture thickens. Pour into individual ramekins and chill.

FIFEHEAD MANOR (B)

Middle Wallop, Stockbridge, Hampshire
Tel: Wallop 565/6
Open 12 noon to 2.30 pm; 7.30 pm to 9.30 pm
Closed Sunday evening

History has left its mark on this lovely old Manor House, parts of which are said to date back to the eleventh century. In its time it has been a nunnery and the home of the Earl of Godwin, husband of Lady Godiva, who is best remembered for her legendary ride through Coventry. Godiva rode out naked, covered by her long hair, in return for cuts in the crippling taxes levied on the town. She had taken the precaution of asking the people to stay indoors; only Peeping Tom disobeyed her and was instantly struck blind!

Today Fifehead is a charming hotel with lovely gardens, comfortable bedrooms (all with private baths) and a candle-lit dining room, where good food and wine are served. The cordon bleu cook has the benefit of home-grown vegetables and local produce, including trout from the River Test. Specialities include the two puddings for which we pass on the recipes – Wim Wam and Chocolate Crumb. The pretty village of Middle Wallop is well placed for sight-seeing – the lovely city of Bath is not far and Salisbury and Winchester with their glorious cathedrals are only ten and fourteen miles away.

RECIPES FROM FIFEHEAD MANOR

Wim Wam

This is a delicious variation on trifle using sponge fingers, Madeira wine and redcurrant jelly instead of the traditional sponge, sherry and raspberry jam, and cream instead of custard.

For 6–7 people
    1 lb (480 g) redcurrant jelly
    ¾ pint (0·42 litres/2 cups) double cream
    ¾ pint (0·42 litres/2 cups) single cream
    1 wine glass of Malmsey Madeira
    2 oz (60 g/⅓ cup) mixed peel
    20 sponge fingers

Melt the jelly over a low heat. Add half the wine. Place half the sponge fingers at the bottom of an oblong dish, pour over half the jelly and allow to get cold. Beat the double and single cream until it's a soft dropping consistency. Beat the rest of the wine into the cream, spoon half the cream over the cooled mixture in dish. Add another layer of sponge fingers, top with the other half of the jelly. Cover with the rest of the cream and sprinkle the top with the mixed peel. Chill in the refrigerator.

Chocolate Crumb

For 4–5 people
½ pint (0·28 litres/1¼ cups) double cream
4 oz (120 g/2 cups) fresh brown breadcrumbs
4 oz (120 g/¾ cup) brown sugar
3 oz (90 g/¼ cup) drinking chocolate
rum to moisten (to taste)
grated chocolate to garnish

Beat the cream till thick but not buttery, mix all the dry ingredients and moisten with the rum. In a glass bowl put a layer of cream, then a layer of bread mixture, until all ingredients are used up, finishing with a layer of cream. Decorate the top with grated chocolate. Chill in the refrigerator. It has a delicious, nutty flavour and an unusual texture.

LA CHARMEUSE GUEST HOUSE (B)

9 Hurst Road, Milford-on-Sea, Lymington, Hampshire
Tel: Milford-on-Sea 2646
Open 6.30 pm to 8 pm
Closed Christmas Day

There can't be too many seaside guest houses in England which serve fresh local trout cooked *au bleu*, accompanied by a bowl of home-made mayonnaise and rolls straight from the oven. Nor too many landladies who leave the puddings on the table for you to help yourself. (Chestnut Gâteau, Crème Caramel with an orange and grapefruit topping or Elderberry Syllabub.) But then La Charmeuse is no ordinary guest house – and its owner is no ordinary landlady!

Born in Smyrna, French-speaking Yvonne met her English husband on a ship in Istanbul thirty-two years ago. England has been her home since 1942.

When her husband died six years ago, Yvonne turned her sea-front home into a guest house with five bedrooms – four with views of the Needles and the Isle of Wight – a dining room facing the sea and a television lounge. Today it has a well-earned reputation for friendliness and excellent home cooking. Most of Yvonne Chamberlain's day is spent in the kitchen. The result is a menu which changes daily and offers a choice of three starters, two main courses and puddings. Although she has a set breakfast menu, she always asks people what they want the night before and cooks it freshly for them.

Her guests tend to stay longer than they planned, like the American couple who came for a night and stayed a week, and many become friends. Someone had just brought her a present of two bottles of elderberry wine made by his wife.

We thought you'd like to try her recipe for Elderberry Syllabub and something called after her grandson – Duncan's Pork Fillet: that's cooking with a personal touch.

RECIPES FROM LA CHARMEUSE

Duncan's Fillet of Pork

For 2 people

1 lb (480 g) tenderloin of pork
1 cup cider ('scrumpy' or dry cider)
12 button mushrooms or larger ones, chopped
12 shallots
1 bay leaf
salt and paprika pepper
pinch of garlic salt
13 oz (390 g) puff pastry (we used frozen pastry)
oil for cooking

Marinade the tenderloin in cider and seasonings for a few hours, preferably overnight. Drain and dry on kitchen paper. Reserve the marinade for the sauce. Brown the tenderloin in hot oil, remove and gently fry the shallots and the mushrooms. Leave to cool. Roll out the pastry and shape into a rectangle. Lay the tenderloin on it, cover with the shallots and mushrooms. Season. Moisten edges of pastry and fold round meat, following its shape. Use small pieces of remaining pastry to decorate the top. Glaze with beaten egg and bake for about 30 minutes at Gas Mark 6 (400°F/200°C).

The sauce:
  1 oz (30 g/2 tablespoons) butter
  1 oz (30 g/¼ cup) flour
  cider from the marinade
  a little stock

Melt the butter gently in a saucepan, remove from heat and add the flour, cook gently for a minute, add the strained marinade, a little stock and cook for a few minutes. Serve the fillet with the sauce and cranberry jelly, or unsweetened apple purée sharpened with lemon juice. (Like all helpings at La Charmeuse, this is very generous. You may find it serves three or even four instead of two, with vegetables!)

Elderberry Wine Syllabub

For 6 people
  1 pint (0·57 litres/2⅔ cups) double cream
  the juice and rind of 2 lemons
  4 oz (120 g/¾ cup) caster sugar
  16 fl oz (0·42 litres/2 cups) elderberry wine
  2 tablespoons brandy or sherry

If you don't make your own elderberry wine you can buy it; Merrydown make it as well as a number of other country wines. Put the cream, the lemon rind and juice, sugar, wine and sherry or brandy into the bowl of your mixer. Put a clean cloth over the bowl and start the mixer at low speed. When mixture has thickened slightly, remove cloth and switch to high until it's a thick creamy consistency. Don't overmix or it will turn buttery. Serve in glasses.

WHITE HORSE HOTEL (B)

Market Place, Romsey, Hampshire
Tel: Romsey 512431
Open 12.30 pm to 2.15 pm; 7 pm to 10 pm

Standing in the heart of the charming market town of Romsey, the White Horse has an elegant Georgian façade which belies its older origins. Inside, there are still traces of an Elizabethan mummers' gallery and rooms with oak beams and Tudor wall paintings. Tradition associates the hotel with Romsey Abbey and indeed it may have been a guest house for the Abbey. The lovely Abbey Church, founded in the tenth century, but mainly Norman, is the focal point of the town which has many attractions for visitors. It is on the River Test, a fisherman's paradise and only five miles from the New Forest with its wild ponies.

On the edge of the town is Broadlands, the home of Earl Mountbatten, where the Queen spent her honeymoon in 1947, and the cathedral cities of Salisbury and Winchester are nearby. Some of the hotel's specialities are traditional English dishes like the recipe below, King Harry's Pot.

RECIPE FROM WHITE HORSE HOTEL

King Harry's Pot

For 4 people
1 pint (0·57 litres/2⅔ cups) fish stock
3 oz (90 g/6 tablespoons) butter
3 oz (90 g/¾ cup) flour
2 oz (60 g) white fish cut into small strips
2 oz (60 g) scampi, cut into quarters
2 oz (60 g) prawns
a little chopped parsley
1 glass white wine
¼ pint (1·5 decilitres/⅔ cup) double cream
salt and pepper

Melt the butter in a thick-bottomed pan, add the flour to form a roux, then slowly add the fish stock (made from the fish trimmings, an onion, a bay leaf and black peppercorns) stirring all the time. When all the stock has been added, let it simmer gently for 15 minutes. Add the white fish, scampi, prawns and the wine. Stir well and bring to the boil, then leave to simmer for 20 minutes. Just before serving add the double cream, the chopped parsley and season to taste.

SOUTH EAST
Kent, Surrey, West Sussex, East Sussex

DRUSILLA'S RESTAURANT (A)

Alfriston, East Sussex
Tel: Alfriston 870234
Open 11 am for coffee; 12.15 to 2.15 pm; 3 pm to 5 pm for tea
Closed November to April, except for teas at weekends
Zoo open all year

Drusilla's is not just a restaurant, more a way of life! Set in the beautiful
Cuckmere Valley, the complex comprises a zoo, a miniature railway, a
farm playground for children, a butterfly collection, a pottery, an
antique shop, craft shops, its own vineyard and wine cellars, its own
bakery and the Thatched House Restaurant. They even produce their
own newspaper, *Drusilla's News*!

It all started in 1923, when the late Captain Douglas Ann opened a
tea cottage on the premises, later adding a pets' corner and miniature
railway. The business flourished and remained in the family's hands.
The pets' corner has become one of the best small zoos in the South of
England; it is under the care of one of Captain Ann's sons. The other
son is in charge of the catering, including the vineyard, which produces
its own Cuckmere Wine.

The Thatched Barn, candlelit in the evening with open log fires, is a
fine setting for the traditional food served there. Especially popular are
the Sussex Feasts with local delicacies, a minstrel and local players providing entertainment during the evening. The bakery produces home-
baked bread, scones and cakes for tea or to take away. Only nine miles
from Newhaven, Drusilla's is as popular and well known to visitors
from the Continent as it is with the locals.

RECIPE FROM DRUSILLA'S

Pippin Pye

This delicious pie, using whole apples, goes back to 1708.

For 6 people

8 oz (240 g/2 cups) plain flour
pinch of salt
4 oz (120 g/½ cup) butter or 2 oz (60 g/4 tablespoons) each of
  margarine and lard
a little water to mix
6 pippins – large juicy eating apples
12 cloves
1 small stick cinnamon
the pared rind of half an orange
2 oz (60 g/4 tablespoons) butter
1 oz (30 g/2 tablespoons) melted butter
1 oz (30 g/just under ¼ cup) caster sugar

Make the pastry by working the fat into the sifted flour and· salt and binding with the water. Leave on one side. Peel and core the apples but leave them whole, put them in a pie dish in which they fit exactly; if necessary put a pie funnel in the middle. Add the cloves inside each apple, the cinnamon and the orange peel over the top and dot the apples with butter. Roll out the pastry and use to cover the apples. Bake at Gas Mark 5 (375°F/190°C) for about 25 minutes. Remove from the oven and brush the top with melted butter, sprinkle with the caster sugar and return to the oven for about 10 minutes.

CAMELOT (A, B)

88 High Street, Ardingly, East Sussex
Tel: Ardingly 892503
Open from 10 am for morning coffee
Lunch 12 pm to 2 pm (last orders)
Dinner 7 pm to 10 pm (last orders; 10.30 pm on Fridays and
  Saturdays
Closed Christmas Day and Boxing Day evening

This privately owned restaurant in the High Street specialises in unusual dishes, carefully cooked by the chef-owner using the best possible ingredients. The restaurant backs on to fields offering lovely views of the rolling Sussex countryside. The village of Ardingly, known to the Saxons as Eithingleigh and to the Normans as Herdingele, has a lovely old church with some very interesting brasses. Mr and Mrs Scholefield, who have run Camelot with a very personal touch since 1972, more recently took over the running of the restaurant at Wakehurst Place.

WAKEHURST PLACE RESTAURANT (A)

Wakehurst Place, Ardingly, East Sussex
Tel: Ardingly 892701 and 892503
Open 10 am to 6 pm for morning coffee, lunch and tea from
Easter to the end of October (11 am to 5 pm in October)

This fine Elizabethan manor house is set in four hundred acres of beautiful grounds. The gardens are associated with the Royal Botanical Gardens at Kew and are used partly as a 'seed bank' and also to grow species which cannot be grown at Kew. The manor house has been turned into offices and laboratories to service the gardens, but two or three rooms are open to the public including the magnificent panelled dining room which houses the restaurant. Here the Scholefields offer very good fresh food with the same personal touch found at Camelot and the same interest in providing unusual dishes for their customers. The restaurant can be approached only through the gardens, to which there is an entrance fee.

RECIPES FROM CAMELOT AND WAKEHURST PLACE

Pork with Cowcumbers

This is the old English word for cucumbers – a nice way to cook pork with a sharp sauce and crisp niblets of cucumber.

For 6 people
  6 loin chops or 12 slices of boned loin
  1 diced cucumber
  2 teaspoons French mustard
  ½ glass dry white wine
  2 pints (1·14 litres/5¼ cups) brown sauce – see recipe for it under
    Tripe and Onions, Drake's Restaurant, London section

salt and freshly-ground black pepper
parsley for garnishing
butter and oil for cooking (or other fat)

Trim off excess fat and sauté the pork in the oil and butter mixture until cooked. Remove from the pan and keep warm. Add the diced cucumber to the juices and cook gently for a minute, add the mustard and the wine and simmer for a further minute, then add the brown sauce and cook for 5 minutes. To serve, pour the sauce over the pork and garnish with parsley.

North Staffordshire Swallows

Let us say quickly that this dish does not use swallows! It's an adaptation of a traditional high tea dish, but makes a very good fish course.

For 6–8 people
  1 lb (480 g) of plaice or other white fish fillets
  2 or 3 medium potatoes, peeled and fairly thickly sliced
  salt and freshly ground black pepper
  fat for deep frying
  lemon and parsley for garnish

The batter:
  ½ pint (0·28 litres/1¼ cups) milk
  4 eggs
  8 oz (240 g/2 cups) flour

Make the batter by combining the eggs with the milk and flour. Leave to stand. Now cut the fish to fit the size of the potato slices, place each piece between two slices of potato and season. With your fingers dip the 'swallows' into the batter, so they are completely coated. Deep fry until golden brown. Allow two 'swallows' per person and garnish with lemon wedges and parsley.

Bells of St Clement's Chicken

For 4 people
  1 chicken
  2 oranges
  2 lemons
  1 medium onion

2 oz (60 g/4 tablespoons) butter
2 oz (60 g/½ cup) flour
about ½ pint (0·28 litres/1⅓ cups) milk
about ¼ pint (1·5 decilitres/⅔ cup) juice from 1 lemon and 1 orange
salt and freshly ground black pepper

Chop the onion finely and sauté it in the butter. Add the flour and stir in the milk and orange and lemon juice, add the zest from one orange and one lemon (keep the other two for decoration). Add the quartered chicken and cook for about 20–25 minutes. When chicken is tender, arrange it on a serving dish, cover with the sauce and decorate with orange and lemon segments.

THE BURPHAM COUNTRY HOTEL (B)

Burpham, Near Arundel, West Sussex
Tel: Arundel 882160
Open from 7.30 pm
Traditional Sunday lunch (to order)

This small and comfortable country hotel stands in a sheltered old-world garden and faces south with lovely uninterrupted views over the South Downs. Built in approximately 1713, with later additions over the years, it has as much character as the lovely village of which it is a part. Burpham, unspoilt and with an interesting and ancient church is only 2½ miles from the historic town of Arundel with its celebrated castle.

Visitors to the hotel will find lovely walks over the Downs, and facilities for golf and riding. A short drive away are the seaside resorts of Worthing, Bognor Regis and Littlehampton offering sea bathing and boating. The hotel has acquired a reputation for very good home cooking – only fresh vegetables are served throughout the year and wherever possible fresh ingredients are used for the carefully prepared dishes.

Roast Shoulder of Lamb with Mushroom and Cranberry Stuffing

For 6 people
  1 shoulder of lamb, boned

The stuffing:
  4 oz (120 g) cranberries
  2 oz (60 g/¼ cup) Demerara sugar
  1 onion finely chopped
  3 oz (90 g) mushrooms, finely sliced
  ½ teaspoon ground thyme
  1 clove of garlic (optional)
  2 slices of bread in crumbs
  chopped parsley
  juice of ½ lemon
  1 egg, beaten
  4 oz (120 g) sausagemeat
  salt and freshly ground pepper
  1 glass white wine
  a little butter and oil for cooking

Cook the cranberries with the sugar in ¼ pint water till soft. Sauté the onion in a little butter, add the mushrooms and cook them gently for a few minutes, add the crushed garlic. In a bowl mix the breadcrumbs, cranberries, sausagemeat, and onion and mushroom mixture with the chopped parsley, thyme, beaten egg, and lemon juice. Lay stuffing onto meat and sew up. Brown the joint in oil and butter, add 1 glass white wine and roast for about half an hour uncovered and for 2 hours covered with foil at Gas Mark 6 (400°F/200°C). Keep meat warm while you make gravy from the juices in the pan.

Blackberry Soufflé

For 5–6 people
  1 lb (480 g) fresh blackberries
  4 eggs
  4 oz (120 g/just under 1 cup) caster sugar
  the juice of 1 large lemon

½ oz (15 g/1½ tablespoons) gelatine
¼ pint (1·5 decilitres/⅔ cup) double cream

Sieve the blackberries through a nylon sieve (you will get about ½ pint of purée). Separate the eggs, put the yolks and the sugar in a bowl and beat until thick and creamy. Put the lemon juice in a cup, sprinkle gelatine over it and warm gently over hot water until gelatine softens. Add the blackberry purée to the beaten eggs, stir in the melted and cooled gelatine. Whip the cream until just thick and fold into mixture. When mixture is just beginning to set, whip the egg whites until light and fluffy. Add egg whites to blackberry mixture, a little at a time, folding in lightly. Pour into a soufflé dish with a paper collar tied round the top and leave in the fridge to set. A few blackberries rolled in caster sugar look nice on top with swirls of piped cream. Remove paper collar before serving.

TRUMBLE'S HOTEL AND RESTAURANT (B)

Stanhill, Charlwood, Surrey
Tel: Crawley 862212
Open 12 noon to 2 pm; 7.5 pm to 9.30 pm (last orders) 10 pm Saturdays
Closed Sunday evening, all day Monday and Tuesday to non-residents

Ten years ago Sue and Peter Trumble turned their own home into a comfortable small hotel. Built in 1872, it's set in two acres of grounds with lovely views. There are only five bedrooms (one with a two-hundred-year-old four-poster bed), all with private bathrooms, so there is a feeling of intimacy and personal service. Charmingly decorated in pastel shades with flowery chintzes, the rooms are centrally heated and double glazed. Gatwick Airport is only a ten-minute drive away, but though you can see the planes land and take off, noise is minimal as the house is at right angles to the runway.

There is a Victorian-style bar and the restaurant offers good English country fare, with everything cooked to order. We choose their Mussels Trumble's Style, Savoury Pork Fillet and Tipsy Bananas as fine examples of good food that does not involve complicated preparation.

RECIPES FROM TRUMBLE'S HOTEL AND RESTAURANT

Tipsy Bananas

For each person
 1½ bananas
 1 tablespoon fresh orange juice
 1 tablespoon sherry
 a sprinkling of brown sugar
 double cream and a slice of orange for serving

Slice the bananas lengthwise, put them cut side upwards in an oven-proof dish, pour over the orange juice and sherry, sprinkle with brown sugar and put under a slowish grill until bananas have softened and sugar is bubbling. Serve with an orange slice on top and double cream.

Savoury Pork Fillet in Mushroom Sauce

For 6 people
 *2½ lb (1·200 kg) pork fillet (it's best if your butcher can bone out
   a leg and cut it in rounds)*
 2 eggs (or 1 egg and a little milk)
 about half a packet sage and onion stuffing
 a little flour
 salt and freshly milled black pepper
 fat for frying
 1 can condensed mushroom soup
 ½ pint (0·28 litres/1¼ cups) white sauce
 2 tablespoons double cream
 ¼ lb (120 g) mushrooms (closed white ones are best)
 parsley for garnish

Flour the pork fillets, dip in the egg and then in the sage and onion mixture, using it instead of breadcrumbs. Fry the fillets until lightly browned. Make the white sauce with butter, flour and hot milk, then mix it with the tinned soup and heat gently until all is amalgamated. Finely slice the mushrooms and fry them in butter. Put the fillet in a casserole, cover with the mushroom sauce and top with the mushrooms. Cover, putting some foil or greaseproof paper under the lid to avoid the meat browning and drying out. Cook in a warm oven, Gas Mark 3

(325°F/160°C) for about 1½ hours until meat is tender. Keep an eye on it to see it's not cooking too fast. When cooked, check seasoning, top with the cream and chopped parsley before serving.

Mussels Trumble's Style

For 4 people
  1 lb (480 g) cleaned and cooked mussels
  2 medium onions
  ¼ pint (1·5 decilitres/⅔ cup) white wine
  1 pint (0·57 litres/2⅔ cups) white sauce
  2 tablespoons double cream
  salt and pepper
  a little cayenne
  2 oz (60 g/1 cup) fresh white breadcrumbs
  garlic flakes
  chopped parsley for garnishing

Chop the onions finely and simmer in the white wine until cooked; add the white sauce (made with 1 pint milk, butter and flour), the seasonings and the shelled mussels. Simmer to heat through, add the double cream and place in individual heat-proof dishes. Sprinkle over with breadcrumbs mixed with the garlic and pop under the grill until brown. Decorate with chopped parsley and serve at once.

CLANDON PARK RESTAURANT (B)

Clandon, near Guildford, Surrey
Tel: Guildford 222502
Open 12.30 pm to 5.30 pm
Closed Monday and Friday

Built about 1733 for the second Lord Onslow by Giacomo Leoni, Clandon Park is one of the finest Palladian country houses in Britain. With its magnificent Marble Hall, fine eighteenth-century wallpapers uncovered during restoration and beautiful furniture, pictures, needlework and porcelain – including a unique collection of Chinese porcelain birds – it offers visitors much to admire.

In common with some other National Trust properties, it also offers simple, but very good freshly-cooked food at moderate prices. Two-course buffet lunches and teas are available in the vaulted dining room. Ingredients are all fresh and bought locally, like the delicious Loseley Ice Cream from Loseley House at nearby Godalming. A very popular choice is the Clandon Pantry Platter which includes English cheese, pâté or pork pie, a tossed salad, French bread and Loseley ice cream. There is also smoked turkey (from a farm in Sussex), rare fore-rib of beef, home-cooked gammon, cold chicken, prawn mayonnaise, pâtés, pies and flans, all served with a selection of imaginative salads. You choose your second course from typical English puddings – fruit pies and flans, trifle and tipsy cake, custards, fools, syllabub and junket. Or you may prefer the cheese board of English cheeses. Tea-time brings a selection of home-made cakes like the delicious Guinness Cake for which we give you the recipe.

RECIPE FROM CLANDON PARK

Guinness Cake

8 oz (240 g/1 cup) butter
8 oz (240 g/1½ cups) soft brown sugar
4 eggs lightly beaten
10 oz (300 g/2½ cups) flour
2 level teaspoons mixed spice
8 oz (240 g/1½ cups) seedless raisins
8 oz (240 g/1½ cups) sultanas
4 oz (120 g/⅔ cup) mixed peel
4 oz (120 g/¾ cup) chopped walnuts
8–12 tablespoons Guinness

Cream the butter and the sugar together until light and fluffy. Gradually beat in the whole eggs, lightly beaten. Sieve flour and mixed spice together, fold into butter mixture, add raisins, sultanas, mixed peel and walnuts. Mix well together. Stir in 4 tablespoons Guinness and mix to a soft, dropping consistency. Turn into a prepared (greased and floured) 7-inch (178 mm) round cake tin and bake in the oven at Gas Mark 3 (325°F/160°C) for 1 hour. Then reduce heat to a cool oven, Gas Mark 2 (300°F/150°C) and cook for another 1½ hours. Allow to cool; remove from cake tin. Prick the base of the cake with a skewer and spoon over the remaining 4–8 tablespoons of Guinness. Keep the cake for one week before serving.

PELHAM ARMS AND SUSSEX KITCHEN (B)

High Street, Lewes, East Sussex
Tel: Lewes 6149
Open 12.15 pm to 1.30 pm; 7 pm to 9.45 pm (last orders)
Closed Sunday, Monday and public holidays

This old coaching inn – it dates back to 1640 – combines a cheerful, friendly atmosphere with very good home cooking. There are fine oak beams in the pub and the kitchen-restaurant is furnished with mellow pine.

Lewes, a charming town in the Sussex Downs, is well-known to music lovers all over the world. It is the station for Glyndebourne, the lovely old house where opera is staged every summer, and where the grounds provide an idyllic setting for picnics in the interval. From the Sussex Kitchen's menu of good English food we have chosen the rich Casserole of Chicken.

RECIPE FROM PELHAM ARMS AND SUSSEX KITCHEN

Chicken Casserole

For 4–6 people
  1 chicken jointed
  8 oz (240 g) mushrooms
  3 onions, sliced
  4 oz (120 g) green or black olives

3 or 4 glasses red wine
½ pint oxtail stock (we actually used a tin of oxtail soup)
a little flour
a little butter for frying

Flour the chicken joints and brown lightly in the butter, remove to a casserole and lightly fry the onions; transfer to casserole, add the chopped mushrooms, olives, wine and stock or soup. Cover and cook in the oven at Gas Mark 3 (325°F/160°C) for 1½–2 hours or until chicken is tender.

SPREAD EAGLE HOTEL (A, B)

South Street, Midhurst, Sussex
Tel: Midhurst 2211
Open 12.30 pm to 2.30 pm (last orders 2.15 pm); 7.30 pm to 9.30 pm (last orders 9.15 pm)

One of the oldest inns in the country, the Spread Eagle dates back to 1430; its 'new' extension was added in 1650! Today you still find candle-light and a blazing log fire in the dining room, open fires in the magnificently beamed lounge and the Four Poster room has an adjoining closet where wigs used to be kept.

There is no lack of modern amenities: the hotel is centrally heated and most of the twenty-seven bedrooms have private baths. The beautiful Jacobean Hall, recently restored by local craftsmen, has the original roof timbers and a minstrels' gallery as well as every modern facility for conferences or private receptions. The grounds run down to a charming old mill pond and part of the hotel overlooks West Street, one of the loveliest in the unspoilt old-world town of Midhurst.

There is a hot or cold buffet lunch in one of the two bars every day of the week and beer from the wood. On Sundays you can have a champagne breakfast with a choice of Black Velvet or Bucks Fizz, scrambled eggs with smoked salmon, Sussex oatcakes with local honey and, in season fresh strawberries and cream.

Chiddingly Hot-Pot

For 6 people
Use chuck steak for this all-in-one family stew rich with the flavour of vegetables and spices.

  2 lb (960 g) stewing steak
  2 oz (60 g/4 tablespoons) dripping
  seasoned flour
  allspice
  salt and freshly ground black pepper
  1 celery stalk, chopped
  1 medium onion, chopped
  1 lb (480 g) potatoes, peeled and thinly sliced
  3 cloves
  1 dessertspoon tarragon
  a little vinegar
  1 oz (30 g/2 tablespoons) melted butter
  ¾ pint (0·42 litres/2 cups) beef stock

Cut the meat into cubes and dust with seasoned flour. Brown meat in the dripping, remove from the pan and fry the celery and onions lightly. Put a layer of onion and celery in a casserole dish, sprinkle with allspice, salt and pepper, cover with a layer of meat and a thin layer of sliced potatoes. Repeat these layers, seasoning and adding the cloves and vinegar. Finish with a layer of potatoes, brush with melted butter. Add stock to come to just below top layer of potatoes, cover with a lid. Cook in the oven at Gas Mark 3 (325°F/160°C) for about 1½ hours. Remove the lid and continue cooking to brown the potatoes for another hour.

Roast Capon and Pickled Pork

For 10–12 people
  1 capon weighing about 7 lb (3·360 kg)
  3 lb (1·440 kg) pickled belly of pork (soaked for 2 hours)
  3 carrots
  3 onions
  1 turnip
  1 swede

2 bay leaves
salt and pepper
butter for cooking
watercress

Peel and dice the root vegetables (leave 1 onion whole for cooking with the pork) put them in the bottom of a baking dish. Sprinkle with salt and pepper. Rub the capon liberally with butter, season and roast in the oven at Gas Mark 6 (400°F/200°C) until bird is cooked, about 2 hours. While chicken is cooking boil the pork in water with a whole onion and two bay leaves. When bird is cooked, remove from tray and keep warm. Make a gravy with chicken stock and juices in the pan, push the cooked vegetables through a sieve and add to gravy. Carve the capon and slice the pork, arrange in alternate slices on serving dish. Garnish with watercress and serve sauce separately.

THE THATCHED HOUSE HOTEL (B)

Warner Road, Selsey, Near Chichester, West Sussex
Tel: Selsey 2207
Open 12.30 pm to 1.30 pm; 7.30 pm to 10.30 pm

'Friends are as welcome by boat as by car' reads the brochure to this friendly small hotel in one of the last real villages in West Sussex. And indeed it is as easy to reach from the sea – the hotel's garden goes right down to the water. You have lovely views of the sea and the Isle of Wight from the dining room, the bar and some of the bedrooms, and there are facilities for boating, sailing or fishing.

Selsey, situated on the southernmost point of Sussex, is twenty-nine miles from Brighton, and only eight from Chichester. The village grew up round a flourishing fishing community which today provides the Thatched House restaurant with the freshly caught sea food which is a feature of their menu – from it we give you the recipe for their Glazed Selsey Crab.

Their comprehensive wine list includes English wines and if you are interested in wine, the hotel arranges special wine tastings; if birds are more your line, then you can have a bird-watching holiday. Children are made very welcome and the owners have created an atmosphere where guests really feel at home.

Glazed Selsey Crab

For 4 people

4 cooked crabs
¼ pint (1·5 decilitres/⅔ cup) white wine
salt and pepper
paprika
2 oz (60 g/1 cup) fresh white breadcrumbs
¼ pint (1·5 decilitres/⅔ cup) cream
6–8 oz (180–240 g/1½–2 cups) grated cheese
1 oz (30 g/2 tablespoons) butter
chopped parsley to decorate

Remove meat from cooked crabs and wash the shells. Put the white wine in a pan and reduce for about 3 minutes, add the butter, salt and pepper and paprika and the crab meat. Cook for about 2–3 minutes, then add the cream and the breadcrumbs. When the mixture has thickened, put it back into the shells. Cover the top with grated cheese and pop under the grill until golden brown. Decorate with parsley and serve.

THE SHANT HOTEL (B)

East Sutton, Near Maidstone, Kent
Tel: Sutton Valence 2235
Open 7.30 am to 9.30 am; 12.30 pm to 3 pm (last orders 2 pm); 7 pm to 11.30 pm (last orders 10 pm)

The Shant Hotel is a study in contrasts. It's a three-hundred-year-old house set in the Kentish countryside, offering modern facilities like a heated outdoor pool and sauna, bedrooms with private bath, telephone and colour TV, a function or conference hall and a private air service to a local air strip. Most of the vegetables are grown in their own market garden and they specialise in traditional country cooking with unusual dishes like the Chicken Britannia, and Honey and Saffron Quiche for which we give the recipes. You can get excellent snacks served with home-made bread in the friendly pub which has real ale, or eat in the restaurant where the bar offers a choice of ninety malt whiskies alone!

RECIPES FROM THE SHANT HOTEL

Chicken Britannia

For 4 people
  2 small chickens
  2 teaspoons salt
  1 teaspoon ground pepper
  1 teaspoon cummin seed
  8 teaspoons English mustard
  ½ pint (0·28 litres/1¼ cups) chicken stock
  fresh breadcrumbs

Cut the chickens in half. Mix the salt, pepper and cummin seed, rub into the chicken pieces. Spread with mustard and cover with breadcrumbs. Place in a baking tin and add stock. Bake in a fairly hot oven – Gas Mark 6 (400°F/200°C) for about an hour, making sure the stock does not dry out. Then baste – but not before the covering has set into a savoury crust on the chicken – and cook for another 30 minutes. Very good hot with savoury rice and the juices from the pan, slightly thickened. But it's also very good cold, a delicious main course to take on a picnic.

Honey and Saffron Quiche

For 6 people
  ¾ pint (0·42 litres/2 cups) double cream
  ⅛ teaspoon saffron
  ¼ pint (1·5 decilitres/⅔ cup) milk
  3 whole eggs and 2 egg yolks
  ¼ pint (1·5 decilitres/⅔ cup) clear honey

The pastry:
  8 oz (240 g/2 cups) plain flour
  6 oz (180 g/¾ cup) butter
  pinch of salt
  1 beaten egg
  a little water if necessary

Make the pastry by rubbing the butter into sifted flour and salt. Bind with the egg and water if necessary. Roll out and line a flan tin. Prick the bottom, line with greaseproof paper and weigh down with beans. Bake blind for about 15 minutes at Gas Mark 5 (375°F/ 190°C). Leave to cool. Make the filling by heating the cream, the saffron and the milk together. Beat the eggs and egg yolks with the honey in a bowl. Slowly add the hot cream, beating constantly with a wire whisk; put back on a low heat and stir constantly over a pan of hot water until mixture thickens slightly. Pour into the cooled shell and bake at Gas Mark 5(350°F/ 190°C) for 25–30 minutes until filling is set. Very good hot or cold.

WOODPECKERS COUNTRY HOTEL (B)

Womenswold, Canterbury, Kent
Tel: Barham 319
Open 7.30 pm to 11 pm (last orders 8.30 pm)
Closed on Christmas Day

What was once a Victorian rectory in over two acres of garden is now a comfortable and friendly hotel with a reputation for serving well-cooked traditional English food. Placed half way between Dover and Canterbury and convenient for Ramsgate and Folkestone, Woodpeckers gets many people travelling to and from the Continent. For overseas visitors it is the first surprising intimation that the English too can cook! And it's the really traditional dishes that visitors keep asking for, things like the Beefsteak and Mushroom Pie in Flaky Pastry for which we give you the recipe.

Pat and Ted Millard who own and run Woodpeckers really take trouble to make guests feel at home – they will even take them on short tours in their 1936 taxi (by arrangement!). Families are made particularly welcome – there are cots and high chairs, baby listening services,

laundry facilities and a selection of children's games. In the grounds there is a heated swimming pool and a swing and sand-pit for the younger ones.

The food is simple, but beautifully fresh, with most of the vegetables grown in the garden and a choice of two or more dishes at each course. The hotel does breakfast, tea, high tea for the children, dinner and a traditional Sunday lunch.

RECIPE FROM WOODPECKERS

Beefsteak and Mushroom Pie in Flaky Pastry

For 8–10 people

The filling:
2½ lb (1·200 kg) best braising steak
1 lb (480 g) onions
8 oz (240 g) mushrooms
3 pints (1·71 litres/8 cups) water
salt and pepper

The flaky pastry:
12 oz (360 g/3 cups) plain flour
pinch of salt
8 oz (240 g/1 cup) butter or 4 oz (120 g/½ cup) each of lard and margarine, mixed
squeeze of lemon juice
about ½ pint (2·27 decilitres/just under a cup) of water (enough to mix)

Cut the beef into coarse chunks, put it in a saucepan with 3 pints of salted water, bring to the boil and let it simmer until the liquid is reduced by two thirds – it will take about 4 hours. In the meantime make the pastry. Mix the flour and salt, divide the fat into four portions, rub one quarter into the flour. Mix to a soft, but not sticky paste with water. Knead well until smooth. Roll out to a rectangle, keeping the edges straight and the corners square. Mark into three sections, without cutting them out. Put a second quarter of fat in small pieces over the top ⅔ of the pastry. Fold the bottom ⅓ of pastry (without fat) over the centre, and the top over the other two. Seal open ends with a rolling pin. Give pastry a half turn, so open end is to your left. Press lightly with a rolling pin to flatten, roll out to a rectangle slightly longer than the first. Repeat this entire process twice more with the remaining quarters of fat. Roll out and fold once more and then put in a cold place for at least half an hour. Complete filling by adding chopped onions and chopped mushrooms (field mushrooms have the most flavour) to the beefsteak. Bring back to the boil and simmer for another 10 minutes. Then leave to stand. Roll out the pastry and give it two more folds. Place meat mixture in a 10-inch pie dish, cover with the pastry, pierce pastry and cover it generously with beaten egg. Bake in a pre-heated oven at Gas Mark 6 (400°F/ 200°C) for 25–30 minutes until golden brown. Serve at once.

INDEX OF RESTAURANTS

HEART OF ENGLAND

EAST MIDLANDS

THAMES AND CHILTERNS

EAST ANGLIA

INDEX OF RECIPES

Also available from Sphere

ARABELLA BOXER'S GARDEN COOKBOOK

With the ever-rising cost of meat and fish, the time has come to replan our menus and to look again at the wide range of possibilities in vegetable cookery. For too long the vegetable has been under-rated, a mere accessory to the meat course, treated with little imagination.

ARABELLA BOXER'S GARDEN COOKBOOK elevates the vegetable to the place it deserves. The aim is to enable the cook not only to recognise the nutritional value of vegetables, but also to enjoy their infinite variety. Vegetable flavours change continually depending on the season; many can be eaten raw as well as cooked, and they can be prepared as juices, salads, soups, casseroles, soufflés, mousses and flans.

An imaginative and remarkably practical book containing over three hundred recipes ranging from the exotic right down to the simple potato.

'For many of us, eating less meat may well become a political and moral, as well as financial necessity . . . so I welcome this large collection of first-class recipes that reveal the range, delicacy and elegance of vegetable cooking' – *The Times*

'Superb' – *Vogue*

0 7221 1798 1   COOKERY   95p

A selection of Bestsellers from Sphere Books

Fiction

TEMPLE DOGS	Robert L. Duncan	95p	☐
RAISE THE TITANIC!	Clive Cussler	95p	☐
KRAMER'S WAR	Derek Robinson	£1.25p	☐
THE CRASH OF '79	Paul Erdman	£1.25p	☐
UNTIL THE COLOURS FADE	Tim Jeal	£1.50p	☐
FALSTAFF	Robert Nye	£1.50p	☐
EXIT SHERLOCK HOLMES	Robert Lee Hall	95p	☐
THE MITTENWALD SYNDICATE	Frederick Nolan	95p	☐
FIREFOX	Craig Thomas	95p	☐

Film and Television tie-ins

THE PASSAGE	Bruce Nicolaysen	95p	☐
STAR WARS	George Lucas	95p	☐
CLOSE ENCOUNTERS OF THE THIRD KIND	Steven Spielberg	85p	☐
EBANO (now filmed as ASHANTI)	Alberto Vazquez-Figueroa	95p	☐
THOMAS & SARAH	Mollie Hardwick	85p	☐

Non Fiction

EMMA & I	Sheila Hocken	85p	☐
DR. JOLLY'S BOOK OF CHILDCARE	Dr. Hugh Jolly	£1.95p	☐
MAJESTY	Robert Lacey	£1.50p	☐
RUIN FROM THE AIR	Gordon Thomas & Max Morgan Witts	£1.50p	☐
THE SEXUAL CONNECTION	John Sparks	85p	☐

All Sphere books are available at your local bookshop or newsagent, or can be ordered direct from the publisher. Just tick the titles you want and fill in the form below.

Name..

Address...

....

Write to Sphere Books, Cash Sales Department, P.O. Box 11, Falmouth, Cornwall TR10 9EN

Please enclose cheque or postal order to the value of the cover price plus:

UK: 22p for the first book plus 10p per copy for each additional book ordered to a maximum charge of 82p

OVERSEAS: 30p for the first book and 10p for each additional book

BFPO & EIRE: 22p for the first book plus 10p per copy for the next 6 books, thereafter 4p per book

Sphere Books reserve the right to show new retail prices on covers which may differ from those previously advertised in the text or elsewhere, and to increase postal rates in accordance with the GPO.

(1;79)